The Board Game

Survival and success as a
company board member

The Board Game

Survival and success as a
company board member

Brian Scanlon & Stephen Schneider

LONDON   MADRID
NEW YORK   MEXICO CITY
BARCELONA   MONTERREY

Published by
LID Publishing Ltd.
6-8 Underwood Street
London N1 7JQ (United Kingdom)
Ph. +44 (0)20 7831 8883
info@lidpublishing.com
LIDPUBLISHING.COM

A member of **BPR**

businesspublishersroundtable.com

Printed in Great Britain by T J International Ltd

ISBN: 978-1-907794-03-2

Cover design: Jose Antonio Menor
First edition: January 2011

Contents

Foreword

Any move into a new position can be difficult. Difficulties may arise from higher required levels of technical or functional competence or from new colleagues or from different criteria for performance. Over recent years there has been an increased awareness of the need to prepare people at all levels for new responsibilities. So considerable effort often goes into the reduction of the risk of failure. Formal and informal training and development often take place and there are growing instances of successful mentoring and coaching processes.

However, when a senior manager is invited on to a Board either as an executive or a non-executive Director, there is a tendency to assume that the past success which has identified the individual will automatically be the basis for good performance on the Board. Management folklore is full of examples where this is patently not true and many new Directors have found the transition far more difficult and complex than they anticipated.

It is widely accepted that the management task has become progressively more difficult, complex and pressurised than ever before. There is also a growing premium not only on the base technical or functional skills required but on the individual's ability to see his or her role in the context of the whole organisation and from a strategic standpoint. To be effective, the manager, as he or she grows within the organisation, is required to develop a range of personal skills – the so-called softer skills – which are, in reality, very hard. These skills should be based on realism and awareness about oneself in relation to others and include communications, influencing, listening and leadership. We all have our own definitions of leadership; often based on those we have seen exercising a leadership function for good or ill. It has been interesting to see how the curricula and syllabi at the leading Business Schools have evolved to address the balance of the functional, the strategic and the personal and, certainly, when I moved from industry to the Directorship of Cranfield School of Management in 1986, I was keen to see the balance evolve so that the real needs of senior management and of organisations and individuals were met in a more relevant and balanced way without losing any focus on the delivery of results.

In this context, the operation of Boards is key to the success of an organisation and, yet, the development of Board members is left largely to chance. As individuals rise to Board level, the factors and qualities which made them successful previously remain important but become secondary to the new "Performance Indicators" which will enable them to succeed on the Board. Millions of words have been written by some very clever and insightful people about management over the years but relatively little about performance and required skills in the Boardroom.

Reading *The Board Game* stimulated me to examine my conscience and to look at my own performance over the years on Boards in the public and private sectors. I find myself puzzling why I spent so much time and effort in the acquisition and review of facts and so little in contemplation of the actual role of a Director and how to optimise my interaction with and influence upon other Board Members. The basic things which I now encourage in people I am advising or mentoring were just not considered consciously enough nor was there any effective process of preparation or mentoring into the new role. I have had to come to the rather rueful conclusion that I could and should, have made a greater contribution.

The common features of situations where I did perform and add value were where I was comfortable with the products, services or markets and at ease with colleagues and with the purpose and culture of the organisation. Where I am less proud of my behaviour was when I took a parochial, defensive posture on behalf of my "patch" for whatever reason, normally a lack of trust in colleagues or the Chairman, and, consequently, failed to raise my game to the organisational level from the personal, from the Divisional to the Board. The role of the Chairman is critical particularly in relation to the CEO but also in terms of getting the best out of the other Directors.

This book, *The Board Game*, written by two such experienced practitioners as Stephen Schneider and Brian Scanlon, is not only timely but useful, as it was for me, in prompting conscious thought on the role and behaviour of the successful Director.

Professor Leo Murray
Retired Director
Cranfield School of Management

Introduction

Joining the plc board is akin to jumping in at the deep end when there is no shallow end in which to practice. This book is written to help prospective directors increase their chances of making a successful transition into the boardroom.

We have found that extensive executive experience is often not enough on its own to guarantee a successful transition. In fact, many new appointees to the boardroom are derailed in the process by exhibiting the very traits that brought them success as a senior executive.

Behaviour, not technical competence, is more likely to determine a successful period of service on the board. Past reputations are of little consequence in a boardroom environment where authority will come more from the abilities to exercise sound judgement and win influence through argument rather than from a reliance on status to command.

Whilst this book has been written with the aspiring member of the plc board in mind, we hope it will also be of value to many established members of the board and their public sector equivalents.

We have used a variety of case studies and excerpts from previously published articles. Some of these have been drawn from a series of commentaries written specially for *Learning & Development* by Stephen Schneider.

Brian Scanlon
Stephen Schneider

London, December 2010

1

The Personal Challenge

It is only natural that successful senior executives will look forward to the day when they are invited to join the board. While there are fewer more powerful signals of professional recognition, there are also fewer greater personal challenges in consolidating a reputation in life. In many instances the transition in roles from senior executive to member of the board will come as a profound shock. Failure to deal with this transition will inevitably be a source of personal disappointment and will not pass unnoticed by other boardroom colleagues.

Often, the very attributes that may have underpinned success as an executive, such as the energetic exercise of authority, can be the very traits that derail additional success in the boardroom. The problem invariably centres on an individual's appreciation of the fundamental differences between task and role and how these are exposed in a boardroom environment. Success comes only when the newly appointed director learns to adopt the right behaviour when performing the tasks of a board member. Ronald Reagan is often described, probably unfairly, as a man of no great intellect but it is very likely that he will command a well respected reputation as President of the United States. With his background as a Hollywood star, he was a person who naturally understood the need to perform the role of President and with his subsequent selection of able ministers he is now perceived to have done an outstanding job.

Joining the board has been likened to being thrown in at the deep end. What is not immediately obvious is that there is unlikely to be any prospect of a gradual entry through the shallow end. It may be an unavoidable reality.

Exposure and Accountability

The personal challenges involved in making a successful transition into the boardroom which have significant behavioural aspects are accompanied by some equally significant changes to issues of exposure. Directors are exposed in a number of important ways.

There is the professional exposure to performance issues. Failure to perform as expected will not only dent a sense personal satisfaction but it will quickly alarm colleagues and lead to expressions of unconcealed disappointment. This is only to be expected at the top team table where politics are ever-present and few concessions may be made during a period of transition. A good chairman should be alert to this and orchestrate the early contributions of a new appointee but this happy situation may well not emerge. Professional exposure can strike at any time and even after a long period of service on the board. The UK banking crisis of 2008-09 was essentially about professional ineptitude and, arguably, the dangers of having professional salesmen take on banking risks. The miscreants may never work again.

The legal exposure of directors now expands inexorably. Apart from issues of compliance and good governance, which are supervised by various regulatory authorities, there is an increasing movement to pursue criminal charges as a consequence of events such as the capsize of *The Herald of Free Enterprise* at Zeebrugge and the Paddington and Hatfield train crashes. Corporate manslaughter convictions may be a reality in the near future.

Quite separately, the financial exposure of directors can easily end in court, too. Limited liability is essentially a shareholder protection and will not shield directors from litigation for damages. Some protection for some corporate failures may be afforded through indemnities that are part of many service contracts but there will be none to protect against fraud or trading when illiquid.

Finally, there is the issue of personal exposure. Questions of integrity, competence, and judgement will be at the core of many boardroom issues. These all affect personal reputation and, indeed, reputation is one of the most powerful weapons that can be deployed by a director. It can transcend all others. How, for example, would one challenge Warren Buffet about views on corporate performance and investment with his reputation at Berkshire Hathaway? Bernard Madoff may have been just as difficult to challenge while he continued to deliver outstanding, if mysterious, returns but his subsequent conviction for fraud has moved all his perspectives into the dustbin. Personal failure may well be the most crushing to bear.

In view of the depth and complexity of exposure issues, it is wise to assume that the accountability of directors is total. There are no hiding places and the general public wants it that way. Excuses invented to shift the burden of responsibility are remarkably weak and transparent and will never prevail. Look at the furore over MPs' expenses in early 2009. Public opinion was enraged as much by the realisation that MPs seemed to suggest that it was not their fault, because they had followed the rules, as it was enraged by any other aspect. Avoiding accountability will be doomed to failure as catching up is only a matter of time.

Some aspects of accountability in the boardroom are collective. Nothing demonstrates the importance of understanding *role* more than this. On the one hand a director should at all times be objective and independent in terms of opinion, yet, when it comes to issues of fidelity and accountability there will be a need for collective responsibility, too. Reconciling apparently conflicting principles, such as individual *versus* collective responsibilities, is one of the joys of boardroom membership! Accepting the concept of total accountability has critical implications for behaviour. It will require a willingness to resign at a moment's notice, without compensation, if a situation warrants it on performance or issues of principle. In less dramatic circumstances, responsibility may be shared to present a united front outside the boardroom. Less obviously, but more frequently, the board must accept responsibility for the activities of an organisation, whether they had any direct involvement or not. Whilst executives can punish subordinates for failure and remain detached, the board has to accept that failure is usually a reflection of its inability to create an environment that delivers success.

Transition

When functional heads become directors there is often a tendency for them to assume that their principal role is to represent the best interests of their function or department at all times. This could not be further apart from what is needed. Representational responsibilities will always be there, of course, but they should never dominate to the exclusion of all else. A new member of the board should seek to become familiar with all aspects of the business. In times of trouble, the law will not discriminate on grounds of expertise or corporate responsibilities when seeking to apportion blame. A new member of the board should also aspire to becoming as capable as any other member in advocating issues outside the strict confines of their own functional portfolio. The trap of pursuing a narrow functionally-driven agenda in an effort to secure some political ascendancy is a major source of boardroom conflict and ineffectiveness.

When joining the board a new appointee will probably have to embrace two new concepts: trusteeship and stewardship. Trusteeship is an active role in corporate affairs, whereby a portfolio of responsibilities is accepted, and it forms the basis of board membership. As a trustee, the objective should be to serve the best interests of the organisation at all times during one's term of service and then to pass on the portfolio to a successor when stepping down. A good trustee will ensure that the portfolio is passed on in better shape that when it was inherited. Stewardship is the equivalent of trusteeship in a voluntary organisation. Here the role will be passive but much more demanding in terms of transparency. As Henry Kissinger is reputed to have commented when at the State Department, "the politics in academia are much more vicious, as the stakes are so low". Trusteeship, although active, is not an executive role. It does not confer authority. This will contrast with any retained executive responsibilities outside the board and will be at the very heart of the transition challenges faced by new directors.

The role of a board member demands an independent contribution based on honesty, objectivity, and best judgement. This contribution has to be made, however, within a framework of collective responsibility. A co-operative style only emerges when there is a powerful bond of trust between members of the board. This may not be a reality nor even possible in many instances. Trust is the result of a constant, natural, and consistent pattern of ethical behaviour in the boardroom. Ethical behaviour is itself the result of adopting a value system which is honest and legal, and which prevails, for example, over all other considerations when unfair or illegal advantage is being justified for short-term expediency. The specific pattern of ethical behaviour in an organisation is a critical component of that most elusive but very real phenomenon known as corporate culture.

The boardroom is a natural arena for taking a strategic perspective. This is far more relevant than having command of operational detail despite the tendency of all people to retreat into the comfort zone of their own expertise when difficult situations arise. One of the Chairmen of British Steel, the very celebrated "Black Bob" Scholey, would enjoy sorting out blast furnace problems at Scunthorpe on the phone in the middle of board meetings and would even take off his jacket and roll up his sleeves! However, he would see its funny side and then reflect on the simplicities of former responsibilities. Strategy is the process of positioning an organisation for future commercial and competitive advantage. It requires a deep understanding of both internal and external affairs and the factors which affect them. Exercising influence over strategic issues is not a simple matter of command. Usually, many strategic issues are outside the control of the organisation and may be subject to very limited influence. The strategic mindset will be more concerned about establishing options for the future and understanding the potential impact of both predictable and surprise events. Successful senior executives are often master tacticians but when faced with their role on the board many will struggle badly with strategic concepts where tangible outputs may not emerge.

Master tacticians will, inevitably, be competent managers. However, it takes leadership to deliver strategic impact. According to the *Oxford English Dictionary*, leadership is the ability to guide by persuasion. It demands the articulation of an argument for action that is so compelling that other people will objectively see its merits and be prepared to act on it. There are few higher accomplishments than the ability to do this. Leadership, however, is abdicated when, as often happens, management seeks only to exert influence through its vested authority. Winston Churchill as wartime Prime Minister was generally regarded as an inspired leader despite a reputation for advancing wild schemes. The historian Andrew Roberts in his book *Masters and Commanders* observes that Churchill never once went against the advice of Field Marshall Sir Alan Brooke, the man responsible for war strategy, if he failed to convince him of an argument. In contrast, Franklin Roosevelt as President frequently overruled his Chief of Staff, General George Marshall, if he saw political advantage. Churchill is seen today as an outstanding war leader and Roosevelt is seen increasingly as a canny machine politician. Interestingly, Roberts believes that Roosevelt's behaviour meant that he might have had the greater political impact because, amongst other things, he failed to understand and address the post-war threat posed by Stalin.

The transition faced by a senior executive when taking up a first boardroom appointment as a director is multi-dimensional. This is summarised for reference in Appendix 1. The differences are deep, subtle, and demanding. It will take time for them to be familiarised and fully absorbed by new directors. The issues are all essentially behavioural and concern the concept of role. Many new boardroom appointees will benefit from mentoring as they struggle with the unfamiliar, suffer the brutal equality that comes with the natural scepticism for reputations that all high achievers seem to project, and smoulder at their inability to win arguments at the first attempt. All new boardroom appointees are urged to make constant reference to Appendix 1. Whenever frustration emerges, the chances are you will not be behaving according to the demands of the role.

Horror stories of the problems of making a successful transition are legion. New board appointments can be made to feel belittled and unwelcome as they get caught in the crossfire when powerful people pursue their personal agenda. The chairman of a major construction company was forced by his board to engage, for the first time in the history of the company, professionally qualified executive directors for the finance and human relations functions. The new HR director arrived feeling very positive and enthusiastic to make his contribution but he failed, for some time, to appreciate the chairman's indifference to his appointment and his refusal to welcome the new arrivals in the way that he should have. The new directors, who were very capable and well qualified, were made to feel, in the words of the HR director, like "new kids on the block". They both went through a very unhappy and unfulfilled period until the chairman was eventually removed. Sometimes the problems can be self-inflicted. When non-executive directors were appointed, for the first time, to a large building contractor one of these new board members, in order to sound convincing in a business where he had little direct experience, fell into the practice of talking at great length about his perspective on operational issues. This was not only a tiresome prospect for his colleagues but it effectively prevented the board from discharging its role as the primary decision making body of the company. The new non-executives had not been prepared for their new roles and the company had made no plans to maximise the impact the new appointments might have. The board only became effective again after the chairman intervened to cure the delinquent director of his desire to justify his appointment.

Life at the Top

What characterises life in the boardroom? It is useful to paint a picture of the scene. Above all, it is important to recognise that it is a political arena. It could not be otherwise and this is perfectly respectable. It should be a forum for constructive compromise. Uncertainties will be the norm. Most surprise events jolt the boardroom, first and foremost. Surprises, by definition, will come with an army of unknowns. The job of the board is to remove the fog with logical and objective analyses and assessments. Ambiguities will be ever present.

The boardroom is the place where all the different and conflicting forces that affect an organisation have to balanced, offset, and resolved. Ambiguity is inevitable when the separate interests of the organisation inconveniently fail to coincide.

Evidence, which is the critical ingredient for the application of reason, logic and the exercise of judgement, will often be scarce. Many attempts to provide evidence will turn out to be little more than hearsay when subjected to critical examination. Popular myth is a powerful reality in many organisations and it is often the responsible for many of the strategic mistakes made by a board. Believing that the destiny of Jaguar Cars was to continue the tradition of the E-type led the company down all sorts of false trails as it tried to define and then fund an appropriate F-type. Its success with the XJ series seemed to be almost incidental while chasing other spectres and the company was left badly prepared to exploit the very market it had created. It took the hard-headedness of Ford to define and produce the subsequent X series and introduce volume production disciplines.

Opinions around the boardroom table will often be divided. Indeed, if this is never so the organisation will be in real trouble! Real opinion may be very difficult to establish at first as many people like to see where others stand before expressing any final views or commitments. Loyalties, which will be ever present but which should not be allowed to intrude on issues of judgement, will be continuously tested in formal and informal ways. In all discussions, human nature will ensure that all participants are constantly assessing where others stand in terms of argument and personal support. Unfortunately, few serious issues ever result in options that are clear-cut. Uncertainty is at the heart of all aspects of life and serious endeavour. Being able to live with uncertainty and mitigate its effects is the hallmark of a true leader.

Finally, conflict of interests will abound and should demand recognition and immediate resolution. These situations, which can be plainly unethical or even border on the fraudulent, can provide some of the biggest and most emotional challenges for a board. Such is life at the top!

The Art of Compromise

The duty of the board is to provide leadership, although this often happens by default. It should attempt to be decisive, unanimous in its call to action, and clear in its communication of intent. It is not only pragmatic, but perfectly honourable, to provide leadership through a process of constructive compromise. Facts and evidence should be well researched, be made freely available, and presented with full transparency. While this is second nature to an objective scientist or a senior military commander, businessmen and politicians tend not to be so rigorous.

The ability to draw valid conclusions separates the wise man from the fool. This is the single most important intellectual attribute in a leader. Sound conclusions are rooted in the analysis of evidence and the absence of evidence will undermine the validity of any conclusions drawn. Falsely drawn conclusions will result in errors of judgement and as such are serious affairs. Once conclusions are drawn they must be given unwavering support and only changed in the light of new or remarkable evidence. This is why compromise is vital when planning action. Agreed action should be the objective output of all boardroom discussion. Action itself should be driven by evidence-based conclusions but it should also reflect the realities of politics, funding constraints, and timeliness. Werner von Braun, the German rocket scientist who masterminded the US mission to put a man on the moon and have him return safely, realised that a successful space programme would be so expensive that it could never be justified as a the unified entity it demanded to be. Instead, he chipped away for years with small budget appropriations to put the fundamentals in place and was never too worried about diversions for military objectives if it meant keeping the overall initiative alive.

When faced with the question as to what he would do with a completely funded programme he was able to convince President Kennedy that it would be possible to have a successful mission to the moon within the decade following Kennedy's inauguration. He compromised in a sensible way at every turn until he could strike and secure his principal objective. Action must always recognise physical realities and political constraints but sound compromise must always avoid taking the path of least resistance or anything that invalidates the policies of the organisation. The western democracies have always taken great pride in the freedoms they offer the individual. It then comes not only as a shock when agencies provide evidence of torture during the interrogation of prisoners-of-war or suspected terrorists but it also quickly undermines international standings and hard won reputations.

The process of compromise is susceptible to conscious and unconscious abuse. Strong personalities, of whom there will be a majority in any boardroom, tend to see life in terms of getting their own way. This is often a simple manifestation of the supreme belief they have in their own judgement. Such people will always deploy the most powerful weapons they have at their disposal to win an argument. They will call in perceived debts for the past support they may have offered. If the debt of support is not recognised, they may then question loyalties or infer moral obligations. Powerful people will not shrink from threatening sanctions, often with a brutal or personal edge, to get their own way. The shock effect of this behaviour when it is experienced for the first time can be shattering for the unsuspecting. This is part of the game to test resolve. A failure to be cajoled by threats may well be followed by a charm offensive and the offer of favours. This can be even more dangerous and distasteful. When a director succumbs to these tactics they become immediately exposed to the continual application of pressure as later issues are raised. Other members of the board will simply resort to the tactic of dividing the opposition to win the day. This is often very effective and may only be evident in retrospect. Who can say that modern management knows nothing about Caesar's *Gallic Wars* even though Latin was lost with the demise of grammar schools! The prevailing sentiment in modern management in reaching a compromise often seems to be that if it is not illegal then it is certainly not unfair.

The only effective weapons to combat unwanted entreaties and pressures are integrity, judgement, and courage. A demand for courage can be daunting. Jim Hacker, the principal character in the television series *Yes, Minister!,* happily justified any colourful reference to his decisiveness except when it was described as courageous. The biggest psychological damage that may be experienced when under pressure in the boardroom is often when one falls into self-deception about an issue or when one acts against one's better judgement. Once damaged in this way a director may be permanently debilitated on the board and end up becoming subservient to the agenda or to a more powerful colleague.

The demands of making a realistic and honourable compromise can throw the most surprising characters in their first boardroom appointments. Macho-style managers can be particularly vulnerable. For a plc board director, authority comes from reputation, respect, and the ability to influence others. The head of operations of a large plc had finally been appointed to the board after many years with the company. He had worked hard as a manager, learning how best to report to his seniors, how to keep them happy, how to impress them, and how to play their politics. He was acutely aware that it would not be an easy matter to get his former masters to treat him as an equal. He planned to mark his territory well and assert his new status at his first boardroom appearance. The big day arrived and he launched into a well-rehearsed monologue on what he planned to do. The board questioned his plans and challenged some of his underlying assumptions. While this was normal fare for the boardroom the new director misinterpreted the questioning as criticism. Believing that the right response was to show that he could "stand-up" to his new colleagues he became both defensive and aggressive. The meeting got off "on the wrong foot" and his first contribution left a largely negative impression. This display of aggressive and intractable behaviour set the tone for the coming months and his entire transition was made very much more difficult as a result.

Why Bother?

The personal challenges in being a director, particularly of a public company, are onerous and substantial. The territory will initially be unfamiliar and new appointees will be exposed to the prospect of failures of a kind never before experienced. An appointment to the board may look like proper recognition for past contributions and achievements but it will come with new risks for professional and intellectual reputations. The best reasons for stepping up to the challenge will probably be around some desire to make a difference for the better. The rewards may be financially attractive, too, but real satisfaction will probably come from a new sense of power and achievement. Beware! This can be a powerful drug.

2 | **Taking up Membership**

In taking up membership of the board, a new appointee should be generally familiar with how the board fits into the organisation and who the main players are. There may well also be an appreciation that issues of compliance and good governance will have to be faced with a new sense of responsibility. What may be less obvious is that the board will be sensitive to external pressures not previously experienced and that it will also have its own difficulties in discharging its duties effectively. In other words, the board will not be a perfect and well-oiled machine ready and willing to spring into action at all times. Part of the challenge will be to contribute to making the board a more effective and relevant institution.

It is important for all members of the board, the new and the experienced, to know what is expected of them when their role changes. A successful CFO of a FTSE 100 company was fast-tracked when the CEO was fired. It was a case of a man being in the right place at the right time. However, he lacked any experience of managing thousands of people and he soon found himself facing all sorts of unanticipated difficulties in exercising his authority and power. Like many extremely bright people, he assumed that most things could be tackled by the application of brainpower. The difficulties he experienced seriously undermined his self-confidence and he became a lost soul. He had completely mistaken his role. He thought his job as CEO was to solve problems, as he had done so successfully as CFO. Again, the issue was about creating the space and place for others to perform.

Context

There are many types of organisation that can be referred to loosely as a company. The main differences between these types will tend to reflect aspects of ownership and liability. The different types can be grouped conveniently into public sector corporations, joint-stock publicly-quoted companies, private companies, partnerships, and voluntary organisations. Collectively, it is useful to regard all these types as some form of corporate entity which will be referred to in this book as a company. The shareholders, such as the taxpayer through a government agency in a public sector corporation and the investor in a commercial company, are empowered to elect a board of management to look after their affairs.

In a company the board will be made up of executive and non-executive directors. The executive directors will be experienced people with significant expertise in one or more functional areas of the organisation. These people wield significant power from the authority delegated to them by shareholders. Individually and collectively they comprise one of the most powerful and influential sections of society. In a partnership the board typically comprises a select group drawn from leading shareholders and it will be usual for all shareholders to be directly involved in the business in some way. Some partnerships, especially the international public accounting and audit practices, have evolved into large corporations. Voluntary organisations, by their very nature, will be very different from those with a commercial mission. Subscribers replace shareholders and lay members tend to represent a variety of constituencies in contrast to directors who simply represent investor interests. Despite the differences and the use of different terminology many of the challenges of being a director will have relevance.

Executive members of the board are usually senior employees of a company and will have a full-time position outside the boardroom. Senior executives typically face the biggest transition challenges when they take up their first boardroom appointment. They will almost certainly be competent and ambitious people who have pursued a career path with some success. Whilst their appointment to the board is not strictly a career path move it will certainly be a major feature of their CV.

Non-executive members of the board are usually only part-time employees of a company. It will be commonplace for these directors to have an executive directorship of another company and they may well have other non-executive directorships, too.

Shadow members of the board will only be found in subsidiary companies. They are usually full-time employees of the parent company and may even be executive directors. Their role is essentially that of a non-executive director.

Culture

Taking up membership of the board will be a different type of experience in different companies. In part, these differences will reflect different commercial pressures and different capital structures. However, organisations also exhibit distinctive, often unique, characteristics that will have evolved over time. This is often regarded as the culture of an organisation and it will be this culture that will largely define the type of challenge that will be faced when taking up a new boardroom appointment.

Organisations can exhibit an infinite variety of behavioural characteristics but, in general, a few key broadly-based types emerge. An organisation is power-centred when its style is authoritarian. Typically, this power will be vested in the strong personality of the chairman or, more likely, the chief executive officer (CEO). Power-centred companies tend to project clear and simple messages at all times. Few employees will misunderstand the direction and priorities set by the board. These companies can be very successful and probably fit the popular conception of corporate life. However, they do suffer serious drawbacks, too. Succession planning can be a difficult proposition. Powerful people tend not to develop immediate subordinates who will have both the skills and the stature to challenge. GEC after years of success under Arnold Weinstock failed to survive his departure. Powerful people will also shape an organisation to suit their own brand of strengths and weaknesses. While this is a natural tendency in all leaders to some extent, in extreme forms it will lead to a structure that may not be logical nor be suited to a successor. Power-centred cultures descend into a cult based on the personality of the person in ultimate control. Southwest Airlines was such a phenomenon and was it a very distinctive experience when it was run by its charismatic founder Herb Kelleher. These situations will put an extra dimension on the challenge of fitting into a board and making a worthwhile contribution.

An organisation is merit-centred when there is a clear spirit of collective endeavour around the board. In these organisations ultimate leadership will follow the more able boardroom performers. The boards of such companies tend to be strong on its functional composition. In these companies, as board members move on, the patterns of power shift imperceptibly as a new personality mix exerts new influence. Merit-centred organisations are much admired and widely copied. Such companies often turn in good, if rarely outstanding, performances but will have the intrinsic flexibility to evolve with changes in the marketplace. Succession issues are usually much simpler to resolve in merit-centred organisations. However, from time to time a new senior player can come from a functional background that can distort values and strategic direction. Accountants will tend to exert a conservative influence when in the top job and, while growth rates may flatten, profits will often advance during their tenure. Conversely, salesmen in the top job are susceptible to growing the top-line in a business without creating a commensurate fall-through to the bottom-line. Successful merit-centred companies often develop a strong core team of executives and their very success and close bonds can be a barrier to full acceptance for new board members.

An organisation is rule-centred when, usually in the absence of noticeable long-term change, power is exercised through an ability to change the rules or conventions. Many rule-centred organisations are in the public sector although with privatisation many of the classic examples, such as the nationalised utilities, have moved on. With its public service ethics and its institutionalised social awareness, a rule-centred organisation tends to adopt management-by-consensus practices. Often, such organisations have very remote commercial objectives and budget management may fill the business vacuum. The positive driving force in rule-centred organisations might simply be avoiding mistakes or at least being always able to justify action in relation to their missions. Succession planning in these organisations can be remarkably simple and effective if rarely egalitarian. Advancement is usually based on merit and service but the candidates, who will often be generalists with deep and shared experience, will have a tendency to perpetuate known and proven models of management.

An organisation is tribe-centred when its performance is determined by the attitudes of a small group outside the formal management structure. Highly unionised organisations, such as the Post Office, usually behave this way. Management may have little strategic impact on activities as change will rest in the hands of people who may see no value in change. Such companies end up in a time warp and will struggle to stay competitive as markets and technologies move on. For this reason, many tribe-centred organisations tend to be monopolies. These organisations present some of the biggest challenges in a modern economy.

Newly appointed directors will not only be faced with understanding their new role and relating it to their other task-based responsibilities, but they will also be faced with making a transition in an environment that will be defined distinctively by the type of organisation culture that prevails. Making a first contribution in a power-centred boardroom will be a very different experience from doing it within a rule-centred top team.

Ethics

Ethics in their simplest form are value systems. They are often adopted by mutual consent in the pursuit of some common cause. Ethical considerations usually result in some declared code of behaviour. Consider the very special circumstances faced by pharmaceutical companies. It would be a catastrophe for them, and their customers, if their research and development programmes were not rigorous enough to reject unsuitable products, such as another thalidomide type offering. These companies need to reward their researchers for developing failures as much as they would for winners, otherwise failures may get out into the marketplace. For these sorts of companies, ethical behaviour has to be hard-wired into the organisation.

In a seminal study on ethics carried out for the Institute on Management Consultants during the presidency of Paul Lynch it was concluded that ethical behaviour was defined by two concepts: transparency and vulnerability. Transparency is not an absolute phenomenon but exists in different degrees. Very cleverly, the IMC study defined degree by the answers to the question," would you reveal this to………? " A low degree results when the answer is "no one" or "selected colleagues" and a much higher degree results when the answer is "to my close and immediate family" Ethical behaviour should have respect for everyone and the test for vulnerability is whether an action affects an interested or involved party in a way that exposes their position and puts them at a disadvantage or opens them to sanctions.

Different value systems cannot co-exist in different parts of the same organisation. This often becomes a problem after a merger or in entering a new alliance. When the dilemma is left unresolved it encourages a process of arbitrage between one system and another until one system prevails. This effect can be seen dramatically in some celebrated cases of police corruption such as the Serpico affair in New York. The driving out process following a merger can feel just as traumatic for those involved.

Continuous and consistently ethical behaviour is the key process in building trust. Trust is consolidated when the value system is respected and its interpretations are predictable. Unethical behaviour is always a shock as it shakes the faith and trust that was formerly accorded. In this sense, the Parliamentary crisis over MPs' expenses in early 2009 was less about suspicions of dishonesty than it was about the collapse of ethical behaviour. Once trust is lost it can be very difficult, if not impossible, to regain.

Constituencies

Organisations, particularly in their extended form, will comprise a number of distinctive constituencies. These can be formal or informal, implicit or explicit. Understanding their distinctive characteristics and needs is critical for effectiveness in the boardroom. A constituency is any important homogeneous grouping that will have some distinctive claims on the organisation that demand constant attention.

Colleagues will form a constituency close to the heart of life in the boardroom. Their views and support will be vital in the decision making process and in the management of change. Additionally, boardroom colleagues will be in the most powerful positions to influence events for the organisation. To become effective with this constituency it important to know as much as possible about their personal leanings, their family values, their social awareness, their leisure time passions, and their working style. All these factors will influence their work ethic, their corporate commitment, their decisiveness, and their personal sensitivities. Understanding the behavioural traits of colleagues is not only essential to help win arguments it is also vital when assessing their judgement. If friendship results, it will be important to maintain objectivity when on different sides of the argument.

Employees probably comprise the most demanding constituency of all. Their well-being will be vitally affected by boardroom decisions and their productivity and cost-effectiveness will be determined by how happily they co-operate in meeting corporate objectives. Employees not only need to feel valued by their organisation and rewarded fairly but they also need to feel that their particular contribution delivers value on their own terms. All tasks comprise the elements of planning, execution, and control. When jobs are defined with one or two of these elements missing there is usually an undercurrent of employee dissatisfaction. It is no accident that some of the most contented of employees have worked under difficult conditions in traditional industries. This is particularly true where the principle of division of labour has little impact on productivity and where working in a close team is normal practice. Miners, for example, work in teams of four or five; they plan their shift in terms of what yardage of coal they will cut; they then move the coal-cutters along the face and plough back the coal won before re-setting the coal-cutter forward for the next shift. The incentive is to maximise the coal won, as that will impact earnings, but come what may the machinery has to be in the right place for the next shift to start without penalty. This all takes eight hours. Now compare this job with its satisfying completeness to that carried out on an auto assembly line where each worker will have two to three minutes of activity to be completed while walking down a 15 metre slot before returning to start again. It may be a competitive imperative but it will create truculence, too.

Shareholders, despite their being so vital to the investment in an organisation, are often a forgotten constituency. However, this is the one constituency that can bite back with some venom. When things go well in a company, shareholders are normally happy to back the resolutions put forward in general meetings by the directors. From time to time shareholders will switch their preferences between taking income and enjoying capital growth according to the state of the economy and their personal circumstances. When things go badly, or when issues that raise questions of ethics or fidelity surface, directors can face a torrid time. Institutional shareholders when suitably motivated can change the composition of a board with almost immediate effect. Disgruntled private shareholders are adept at frustrating resolutions put forward by directors and will enjoy subverting executive remuneration proposals when provoked. A good chairman will always be sensitive to shareholder interests at board meetings.

Colleagues, employees and shareholders represent the traditional core constituencies of an organisation. In highly unionised companies there is always the danger that if the union replaces the employees as a prime constituency the company can get progressively divorced from their employees. However, in highly unionised organisations the employees will certainly not be a forgotten interest group even if they get very detached.

Outside the core, customers and suppliers represent important commercial constituencies and with a growing emphasis on customer service and more extensive outsourcing practices these constituencies have an increasing relevance. Customers provide the only non-financial revenues for an enterprise and their requirements will drive business opportunities. A common axiom in business is that the *customer is always right* which should signal their importance if nothing else. Customers should always be accommodated whenever possible but should never be allowed to get so close that they can influence directly the allocation of vital and scarce resources. Customers can be ruinously expensive unless positioned on the right terms. Suppliers, with their willingness to extend credit and their contributions to quality and innovation, underpin the whole business. It is now increasingly common to speak of suppliers as partners although relationships are more likely to be contractual than ones of ownership. Suppliers who do not produce goods for end-users are particularly vulnerable to the success of their principals and deserve to be part of business planning exercises. With pressures on cost containment it is all too easy to pass on the pressure to suppliers. If this results in the failure of the supply chain little will have been achieved. The major supermarket chains in the UK have managed to destroy the domestic dairy farming business through over pressurising farmers on prices and they are now exposed to the volatile behaviour of continental farmers.

In recent years there has been a growing use of the term stakeholder. This new term embraces two increasingly important constituencies in the shapes of the general public and the government. With a growing and often quite sophisticated awareness of environmental issues the general public already drives the affairs of some companies. Nuclear fuels re-processing and new motorway construction come in for particular attention. This involvement with the general public can be very political and often unwelcome but it cannot be ignored. The government in different guises can often be a customer, a supplier, a regulator, and on occasions a competitor. These circumstances no doubt inspired the very American sentiment that *you can't beat City Hall.* In these roles, government must be treated as part of whichever constituency is relevant despite any calls they may table for special consideration. However, governments can change the rules of the game and will set the burden of taxation. To make matters worse, government through its agencies may not behave rationally or consistently and is impervious to most attempts to punish. Anticipation and avoidance action are the best weapons to combat government interference.

Finally, there are also parties who will seek to impose themselves on an organisation as a legitimate constituency to further their own agenda. Such parties may include the media, pressure groups, and single-issue protagonists. Some of these parties may even have charitable status. All have to be handled with care and it is worth remembering at all times that many will have no legitimate claims for consideration.

All constituencies are better managed through co-ordinated programmes of internal and external relations. All members of the board should be competent in articulating the policies of the company to any enquirer and be comfortable in doing so. Nothing is likely to be more testing for a director than being required to do this alone and at short notice. It is a useful exercise for all directors to rehearse what might be said about objectives, activities, and policies to a constituency with a claim on the company.

The way constituencies are managed in a company will often define its public image. These images can be very valuable and powerful but when they are at variance with reality severe problems can result.

Roles

Playing a role is very different from undertaking a task and the boardroom is essentially a place bound up in roles.

The chairman is the nominal head of a company and this defines their primary role. Their main responsibility, however, is to look after shareholders' interests. A powerful chairman will be able to fire the CEO unilaterally if that is deemed to be in the best interests of the shareholders. Such a move would be infrequent, of course, and only in the event of a very serious situation arising. In doing it chairmen would almost certainly seek the unanimous support of their non-executive directors. If this action were not ratified by the next general meeting the chairman would be obliged to resign. The day-to-day activities of the chairman will concern preparation for and the conduct of board meetings. This work may vary enormously in scope and content from one company to another but it will almost certainly include the preparation of the agenda, the collation of papers for submission, and the drafting of minutes with the assistance of the board secretary to summarise the outcome of meetings. It is the sole responsibility of the chairman to build the board, subject to eventual shareholder approval, so as to secure the objectives set for the organisation in a most effective way. This building activity should include executive and non-executive directors. A board should consider itself to be a sovereign body in the sense that there will be no higher authority in the affairs of the company. In association with the CEO, the chairman should set corporate strategy and should expect to be given a budget sufficient to prepare strategic plans comprehensively and objectively.

While the chairman is the statutory and nominal head of an organisation, it is not unusual for leadership to reside effectively with the CEO. Indeed, in the USA this would be normal practice. However, this is not an ideal situation for British practices. Despite corporate governance codes that promote a division of responsibilities between chairman and CEO, some companies allow the posts to be combined. Surprisingly, Marks & Spencer, which is often cited as a model of British enterprise, sanctioned such a move with the appointment of Stuart Rose.

The chief executive (CEO) is responsible for the use and deployment of company resources including capital, property, plant and equipment, and people. The principal objective of the CEO is to deliver profits from the best use of corporate resources. It is the sole responsibility of the CEO to build an executive team in a way that parallels that of the chairman in building the board. Often, the strong personality of the CEO when combined with the power derived from their being in control of all budgets can lead to many CEOs being the *de facto* head of their organisation. Tensions between chairmen and CEOs are ever present and most organisations experience the backwash of a power struggle. This may not be how it is supposed to be but it is in the main the reality even when CEOs are powerful enough when constrained by statutory rules and the codes of good governance. With the power of patronage that comes from building an executive team the political power of CEOs is immeasurably strengthened by strong loyalties. It takes a chairman of great stature to rein all this in.

Within the executive team the finance director (CFO) has a special role to fulfil as official scorekeeper. Numbers increasingly drive modern businesses and the CFO is charged with underwriting the integrity of performance numbers for the board, the shareholders, the regulatory authorities, and the tax authorities. This is essentially a statutory role. Additionally, the CFO will be charged with producing management accounts that compare outturns against budgets and allow operational judgements to be taken. Of necessity, the CEO and the CFO will work closely together and their partnership often appears to speak with one voice. A CFO rarely expects to be challenged on fundamentals by other directors. This is usually because financial matters are supposedly opaque to all but qualified accountants. Being competent enough in financial affairs to challenge the CFO should be a key objective for all directors. Conversely, many CFOs take a very detached view of the other non-financial activities of the company and will have stronger affinities with their opposite numbers in other organisations than with other members of the board.

In former times, a special place was reserved on the board for the company solicitor or a general counsel. Today, the duties associated with these roles are carried out by the company secretary. Too often now, the role of company secretary is appended to that of the CFO and this can be a little too cosy to serve the shareholders' best interests. A company secretary will be responsible for keeping the shareholders register, submitting returns to Companies House, supervising compliance issues, and keeping the conscience of the business. Effective company secretaries can have an enormously beneficial impact on the affairs of a company.

Other executive directors face their biggest challenge in putting in effective management performances. They are often the junior players on the board but with the support of the CEO they can wield substantial power. Executive directors often fail to fulfil their wider role and many will retreat into a functional comfort zone. Indeed, many executive directors, particularly those who tend to see their directorship as some kind of reward, take the view that much of the board's agenda is of little direct interest to them. These are the sort of people who would be best confined to the executive committee as they have little to contribute to the direction of the company. However, the executive director group on the board also represents a great potential opportunity for an organisation. Motivated, open-minded, and enlightened executive directors will transform a company.

Non-executive directors have a critical role to play in keeping the ring between the chairman and the CEO, in bringing external experience into play, and in forcing objectivity into discussions at all times. They have a particular role to play in ensuring good governance and compliance. Sadly, many non-executive directors are a disappointment. Above all they should be alert to the dangers of gross error and they should act as a check on over powerful chairmen or uncontrolled CEOs.

However, it is not uncommon for non-executive directors to avoid these difficulties and treat their positions as a sinecure. The corporate failures of the 200-09 banking crisis in the UK were essentially their failures to contain over-ambitious and under-endowed CEOs.

The Board

A board will be a mix of different personalities, a galaxy of different talents, and an apology of misunderstood roles and relationships. As an entity it also has a number of roles to discharge.

The board must take authority for the preparation of a strategic plan. This plan should attempt to position the company advantageously with respect to its markets and its competition; it should anticipate and then counter any threats its existence; and it should continuously align its structure to deliver results in an effective way. Many boards get distracted by the urgency of current events and the excitements of intervention. This sort of behaviour reduces the board to being just another version of the executive committee and will destroy its essential utility. The board is the only forum available to establish and develop the capital structure of the organisation. It needs to ensure that adequate funds are raised through an appropriate issue of shares and debt instruments; it has a critical part to play in declaring a dividend; and it must programme expenditure on capital projects. With such a canvas members of the board should be inspired but too often the challenges fail to deflect the self-indulgent pleasures of being a member of the top team. A board works best when its members continuously search for improvement and opportunities, rigorously apply objective analyses and assessments at all times, and look to employ sound judgement based on experience and ethical values.

It is now regarded as good practice, with good reason, for boards to set up a number of key committees that comprise non-executive directors, to promote good governance. An audit committee, which should work independently of the executive but in close association with the statutory auditors, is essential to ensure the fidelity of results and accounting practices. The remit for the committee should have few, if any, constraints and it should have access to a budget sufficient to probe hard in vulnerable areas. Even in well-run companies the audit committee should be constantly exposing all sorts of embarrassing situations. A quiet audit committee will be sitting on a nest of poor practices and disciplines. Ideally, the committee should be chaired by the senior non-executive director and have access at all times to the chairman and CEO.

A remuneration committee should be active to determine the compensation arrangements for all executive members of the board. Unfortunately, the majority of these committees have not yet delivered the benefits anticipated when first introduced in the mid 1990s following reports on corporate governance. This may be about to change. While many committees sanction expenditures to participate in compensation comparison studies, few have been brave enough to rein in excessive packages. There has been a tendency to treat executive directors as the owners of a business with their own capital at risk and significant proportions of the growth in profits have been diverted into executive bonuses. In 1945 a director's compensation was typically 15 times that of the lowest paid. By 2008 some companies had reached factors of 350 times. Remuneration committees have at their disposal a powerful spectrum of payment options in terms of basic salary, share options, pensions, and bonus payments. A major challenge following the difficulties of financial institutions in 2008-09 in the UK is to configure bonus payments in such a way that long-term performance is secured before bonuses are confirmed.

A nominations committee should be present to provide the board with a current list of prospective candidates to join the board to maintain its continuity and forward development. Prospective executive directors will usually be nominated to the committee by the CEO. Prospective non-executive directors should be identified through proper search procedures and budgets should be set aside to do this. In large quoted companies most current non-executives will, unfortunately, have been chosen from a narrow group of fellow non-executives. This often underlies their generally disappointing performances. It is a case of the framework being sound but the application leaving something to be desired. The next generation of directors need to address such shortcomings in current boardroom practices as part of their commitment to make a difference and add value.

Compliance

Failures in business practices since Edward Heath first talked about the unacceptable face of capitalism have prompted initiatives to set out guidance on good governance. Starting with the Cadbury Report in 1992 the UK has built up an impressive and comprehensive code of corporate governance. While its application is essentially voluntary, few quoted public companies will be in default of any of its main provisions. Companies seeking public flotation are obliged to adopt the provisions now as a pre-requisite of funding by public subscription.

Compliance is outside the scope of this book. Newly appointed directors are now invariably placed routinely on induction programmes that address compliance. Many organisations, such as the Institute of Directors, provide excellent tuition programmes to keep directors abreast of implications. The subject is central to good governance and a summary of the key legislation embracing compliance and good governance is provided in Appendix 2.

Due Diligence

When taking up a new boardroom appointment it is important to do some basic homework on what is on offer despite the excitement of a new challenge. A consultancy providing coaching services used an executive search company to find a new managing partner to join its team. The position was sold aggressively and a candidate with a good track record was appointed. Within weeks the new managing partner concluded that the business model was not convincing and did not fit with his experience and expectations, leaving him with an uncomfortable feeling. When he was able to analyse more deeply the financials, which had not been made fully available to him before his appointment, he was horrified by what he found. Rather than pursue a case of misrepresentation he took the courageous decision to resign there and then.

3

Key Attributes for Success

In many ways the transition from senior executive to director is encapsulated by the contrast between a task-focussed position and that of a role-centred responsibility. Personal attributes are likely to be more important than technical skills in measuring success.

Political Power

The ability to influence is central to a successful appointment as a director. The keys to exercising influence are the use of power and politics. Politics, outside the purely political sphere, is often considered to be unnecessary, distasteful, and counter-productive. In some cases this may be a fair summary but the reality is that politics are inevitable and essential for honest compromise, which in turn, is part of the decision making process.

Politics is the exercise of power through persuasion when dealing with people and organisations. Its purpose is to influence the outcome of events. It is constructive when the attempts to influence are based on sincerely held views; it is destructive when influence is sought to gain personal advantage over more objective positions. Political power and influence in the boardroom comes from aspects of behaviour and authority. Authority itself is derived from the position a person occupies in the chain of command and is augmented by personal stature and reputation. Effective authority relies on respect and has to be earned; reliance on position alone is insufficient. Appropriate behaviour, that is playing the part in the way that is expected, will consolidate a person's authority and increase their political effectiveness.

When power and authority are derived solely from a person's position in the chain of command it may offer short term results but will almost certainly be ineffective in the longer term. If a call to action is not supported by arguments that are clear, credible, and compelling the resulting outcome will inevitably be compromised or debased. Those that habitually hide behind position to impose action tend to become marginalised as boardroom players. For example, the exercise of authority without apparent reason, in cases of minor motoring offences, is a key reason for the growing disillusionment of the law-abiding middle-classes with the police.

Power is easily abused. While powerful individuals in positions of influence can be a beneficial force for change, they can also be at the root of catastrophic misjudgements if they are not effectively challenged. In recent times, the performances of Sir Fred Goodwin at RBS and Adam Applegarth at Northern Rock demonstrate what can happen when people, working outside their areas of professional experience, exercise reckless judgement in the assessment of risk. Judgement is the bedrock of good leadership and failure here, when exposed or discovered, is almost impossible to survive, especially if the leaders enjoy a high profile in public.

Authority derived from personal stature and reputation is probably the most powerful of all. When it is supported by sound argument it can sway the undecided and the unconvinced. Only Archbishop Desmond Tutu could have proposed a Truth and Reconciliation Commission in post-apartheid South Africa to heal the wounds of the past. It remains a unique initiative despite the emergence of many more situations where it might have been called for. Stature and reputation are sustained in organisations by the continuous exercise of sound judgement. This is a demanding challenge. Conversely, a sustained period of consistently poor judgement will destroy even the greatest reputation.

In adversarial societies, such as the English-speaking world, arguments based on facts and evidence will have a big impact on decision making. In these circumstances, good politics will be about the construction of compelling arguments that are presented in a way that will have the desired impact on an audience. Effective and admired politicians are invariably highly skilled in the arts of advocacy and sometimes are accorded the status of being statesmen.

Influence in the boardroom will often be the result of a network of inter-related loyalties. This is tactically very powerful for those that command the loyalties but, as loyalties change with issues and events, so the patterns of influence change, too. Shifting patterns of loyalty are the reason for most boardroom power struggles and fewer things can be more damaging than this for an organisation. Influence can sometimes be exercised through unusual, and sometimes worrying, forms of dependency. Nature abhors a vacuum and will conspire to fill it. So it is in business when there are weak executives in senior positions. The CEO of a large public sector transport undertaking became over-dependent on a capable but very dominant HR director who shielded him from difficult issues in industrial relations. This over-dependence was very obvious to many other senior executives and highly resented. While the HR director was distrusted as a natural conspirator with far too much influence for her position she was powerful enough to distort the whole chain of command into reporting through her to the exclusion of the CEO. The HR director happened to be a very capable and remarkably objective force for the organisation but it suffered badly from its weak leadership because the surrogate leader could only ever exercise a narrowly-based perspective from her position.

Power is often considered to be a drug. Certainly, abuses of power are quite commonplace. Winning arguments and exercising influence can be very exhilarating. The responsible use of power demands a conscious effort to be objective at all times and this objectivity, with the courage to maintain it in the face of opposition, is the only antidote to the abuse of power. Power comes from a combination of leadership, professionalism, relationships, trust, and judgement.

Leadership

Leaders are people who attract followers. They tend to behave in a way that underwrites the uncertainties of others. Their drive may be based on a personal desire to intervene in affairs when their own values, beliefs and skills are perceived by them to offer better solutions to problems. As Shakespeare observed that some men are born great, while others have greatness thrust upon them, so it can be with leadership. One of the most notable Lord Mayors of London in recent times was Sir Francis McWilliam who knew exactly what was needed in response to the terrorist bombings that devastated the City during his term of office; business continuity in the face of outrage through the immediate availability of alternative office accommodation and access. It disrupted his plans for his Mayoralty but made his reputation.

Followers can be driven to follow as much as leaders are driven to lead. A highly effective operations director showed unusual commitment to both her work and her boss, the managing director. When, following an acquisition, the MD became much less available for the operations director on a day-to-day basis, the dynamic of their relationship changed dramatically. Suddenly, the employee who had been so eager to please became distant, aggressive, and intractable. On a rational level things were the same. She understood where the company was going, was clear about her role in that future, and was content with her status. However, at an unconscious level the situation had changed dramatically. The operations director had idealised her boss because, while he had time to nurture her, he represented all she had never had in her relationship with her father. The moment his focus changed due to the acquisition he became the "bad father" of her childhood and all the past difficulties of that relationship were projected onto him. This kind of transference is a common occurrence in leader/follower dynamics. The MD found time to re-engage with his operations director when he was made aware of the issue and, as a mark of true leadership, recognised that at the top the job became as much about the performance of others as it about his own.

Leadership qualities should emerge in response to challenges and they can be developed through participating in structured programmes and through experiential learning. Coaching is a process that can transfer skills, advice, and the benefits of experience. Successful leaders often have access to a number of coaches who will rehearse with them the different options they might engage with when meeting specific challenges. As Prime Minister, Mrs Thatcher had access to people such as Professor Alan Walters who was a constant point of reference in the application of monetary policies for the management of the British economy.

Counselling is a process that explores the causes of negative behaviour when the negativity comes from natural instincts. Its objective is identification and correction. When emotional preferences and logical choices are in serious conflict negative behavioural traits will emerge unless there is access to good counselling. This can be very formal, as in the case of serious criminals, or very informal, as in the case of using trusted and objective friends or colleagues as a check against gross errors. Mrs Thatcher again provides an illustrative case in the way she encouraged Lord Whitelaw to drag her back from positions that ran the risk of being too extreme.

Mentoring is a process of exploring new ways of doing things especially when behavioural or institutional barriers would otherwise inhibit progress. Good leaders are always big enough to accept mentors and value their contribution. Mentors help the personality adapt to fit the challenge of the role. Harold Macmillan appears to have been a mentor to President Kennedy when he was being frustrated by Soviet political intransigence early in his term. If this helped him to be more decisive over the Cuban missile crisis it will have been one of the most significant acts of political support in modern history. Good leaders are big enough to change their mind when faced with new evidence and sound arguments. A new, young CEO arrived at a major financial institution, full of ideas and anxious to make his mark. His task was to save an ailing company. Moving swiftly, he laid down plans to bring in fresh blood and failed to recognise the risk that too many new faces would lead to "tissue rejection". He had failed to recognise the irreplaceable performers that often sit quietly deep inside the organisation. When, after some mentoring, he took the trouble to explore existing talent he came up with a very successful blend of the old and the new.

Leadership is often confused with management. Management is the process of making happen that which is agreed whereas leadership is the process of making happen that which is needed. Leadership demands the pursuit of a strategic vision that transcends personal ambition. This is where the leadership of so many financial institutions have now been seen to fail as they have pursued the maximisation of their income to the exclusion of all else. Good leaders will be decisive when situations may be plagued by uncertainty and ambiguity and simply their getting more things right than wrong will guarantee their success. Good leaders will provide clarity for their colleagues and win the commitment of the members of their team. Working with good leaders provides opportunities to learn, improve, and take on more responsibility.

A good board will comprise a group of leaders committed to a common cause. A weak board will be a collection of powerful personalities with each seeking hegemony or advantage. Powerful personalities who avoid the responsibilities of leadership will inevitably clash whereas true leaders will find the sort of compromise that is essential for constructive co-operation. The qualities that underpin leadership are giving to others rather than demanding of them, understanding consequences rather than being knowledgeable, and being able to influence people rather than hiding behind rank.

Professionalism

Professionalism is the pursuit of uncompromised delivery within an ethical framework of behaviour. It embraces a commitment to getting things right first time and this is, perhaps, the hallmark of a true professional. People regarded as consummate professionals are often credited with a form of selfless dedication that is held in high esteem. The attribute is not won through mere qualifications but has to be earned. It requires objectivity and independence at all times and often comes with the obligation to offer leadership whenever none is forthcoming.

There is a hierarchy of interests in the provision of services that lays a foundation for professionalism. The customer or client must come first in all considerations. The professional firm must come second and personal considerations should always come last. This is a hard regime to apply but it puts professionals beyond reproach and soon becomes a way of life.

In more recent times, a more cynical definition of professionalism has emerged. It is exemplified by the professional foul committed by sportsmen to prevent opponents gaining advantage. This alternative sense is also creeping into business but it has no place there. A good professional will prepare well for new situations and attempt to anticipate the possible range of outcomes and events. This is part of the process of avoiding unnecessary and unwelcome surprises and being best prepared for all eventualities. Professionalism should grow with experience and makes an important contribution to cost effectiveness in business. The qualities that underpin professionalism are objectivity, independence, and ethical integrity.

Building Relationships

Whereas intellectual intelligence drives competence in analysis and the construction of a thesis, it is emotional intelligence that drives the formation of relationships between people and their organisations. Relationships are the foundations for teamwork, alliances, and contract negotiations. Good relationships will result when the different parties involved in a situation recognise their relative positions, accept their respective responsibilities in working together, and prepare channels to agree on how to move forward collectively. In the absence of good relationships communications between different parties become more difficult and misunderstandings become more prevalent.

Teamwork is critical in modern business activities. It accommodates the contributions that can only come from different specialists, it spreads the workload, it provides a broader basis for the assessment and mitigation of risks, and it builds commitment through participation in decision making. Team building skills are vital for members of the board. Indeed, the reputation of the Chairman will ultimately rest on an ability to build a team for the boardroom. Inter-personal relationships often drive the true effectiveness of a team and it will be a matter of the team leader's judgement as to whether the different participants can be made to work together effectively. President Johnson built his cabinet on the principle that it was better to have his main dissenters inside the tent than to have them outside and free to cause mayhem, although he described the process in more colourful language. In contrast, Alf Ramsey dropped Greaves, his leading goal scorer, for the final of the World Cup because he did not fit well into the style of play he wished his team to employ.

Good external relationships are as important as good internal relationships in an organisation. The special sensitivities that come with external parties usually mean that diplomacy should prevail over the simple exercise of authority. External relations are increasingly seen by modern organisations as the responsibility of specialist departments. The workloads involved, particularly since the narrow concept of responsibility to shareholders has been widened to responsibilities to stakeholders, inevitably make this a growing practice.

Negotiation is a critical component of all relationship building whether or not a formal contract is the result. It is a process of recognising the positions of other parties and finding common ground so that progress towards complimentary objectives can be made. Formal or informal contracts are the usual result of negotiations. In adversarial societies negotiations are often, but mistakenly, seen as games with a win-lose outcome. In parts of Asia there is often a more powerful desire to find win-win outcomes.

Many relationships will become crystallised in a formal contract. While this may lack a certain degree of flexibility it may have compensating benefits in terms of risk containment. In all cases, disputes over contract are better settled through an agreed process of arbitration than by litigation.

Alliances will emerge when independent parties have a clear common interest. Such arrangements are essential with suppliers but are unethical, and probably illegal, when made with competitors in the form of a cartel. Alliances are usually the result of negotiation and enshrined in a contract. However, all alliances should be valued by their utility alone and should be terminated, without rancour, if changed circumstances eliminate the benefits. Lord Palmerston once observed, as Foreign Secretary, that Britain had no permanent friends and no permanent enemies; it only had permanent interests.

The qualities that provide skills in relationship building and negotiations are being a good listener, exercising fairness at all times, and diplomacy in addressing sensitive issues.

Building Trust

People who are trusted have an extra weapon in their armoury in the fight to persuade or influence. Trust can swing opinion more powerfully than argument alone. However, it is a perishable commodity and cannot be faked despite the continuous assault of rogues and fraudsters. Trust empowers people and, at its best, will often simplify relationships without making them vulnerable. It comes from continuously ethical behaviour and the consistent application of sound judgement. It is always earned and can never be demanded; it takes time to build and it can be lost in an instant of recklessness. When trust is common currency around the boardroom outstanding performance usually results. It is the basis of honest and objective debate; it underpins all personal influence; and it helps to mitigate risks through a process of sharing the burdens of decision making.

Directors are, effectively, trustees appointed by the board with shareholder approval to look after, to best of their abilities, the best interests of a company or organisation. The qualities that comprise the foundation for trust are integrity, transparency and selflessness.

Judgement

It is axiomatic that without judgement all else is worthless, especially in the boardroom. As is often the case, evidence for action can be incomplete, absent, or ambiguous. In such cases judgement will have to substitute for deterministic analysis. Exercising good judgement comes from mobilising experience. It is essential, in different situations, what the test of judgement ought to be. For example in criminal law the test is *beyond reasonable doubt*; in civil law the test is *on the balance of probabilities*; in science it is *known to have satisfied all recorded observations and successful in predicting new events*; and in the US Constitution it is *what the Founding Fathers probably intended.* Few organisations will be able to set out their various tests in such precise terms and, unfortunately, the subject is rarely discussed. This is why judgement calls frequently create dissent as board members subconsciously apply different tests. This often leaves judgement calls to be proven long after events when objective analyses can be carried out.

Every organisation will seek some balance between untrammelled enterprise on the one hand and crushing conservatism on the other. This balance, whether implicitly or explicitly derived, will help define the image, style and culture of an organisation.

Judgement must be separated from decision making. Although all decision making should be based on sound judgement, expressing a judgement is more likely to impose a constraint or an objective rather than constitute a decision.

4

Adding Value

Boards can expect to come under ever increasing levels of scrutiny from their shareholders, the media, and their own subsidiary operations. Difficulties will inevitably arise if boards are seen more as cost centres than as a source of value. This can be particularly true when operating authority has been largely devolved to divisions or quasi-independent subsidiaries.

All directors need to understand how to add value for stakeholders through discharging their boardroom re-sponsibilities.

The Vehicles

There are four principal vehicles for adding value in the boardroom.

Leadership comes first. This starts with having a clear vision for the future of an organisation which is focussed on building sustainable competitive advantage for products and services in selected markets. It will require the ability to influence other boardroom colleagues when facing critical decisions and events. Typically, the uncertainties thrown up by continuous change put constant pressures on leadership. In a forum of equals, such as the boardroom, leadership comes from a mixture of personal stature, a reputation for sound analysis, and effective advocacy. Influence will grow with experience and its value to the organisation lies in the way a director can unify the separate efforts of others in a common cause. However, while leadership is a necessary contribution to success it is not sufficient in itself.

Objectivity is a second vehicle for adding value in the boardroom. For individuals it requires putting the wider interests of the organisation above issues of personal advantage. It will demand a sense of realism about events and circumstances and a commitment not to avoid difficult or unpleasant situations when they demand attention. Objectivity is a duty for directors. Its practice can be a powerful antidote to the abuse of political power or position by other boardroom colleagues. Shareholders, who will represent a wide spectrum of different interests, are normally very alert to situations where members of their board might have been less than objective.

Integrity is a third vehicle for adding value. It is a mixture of honesty, fidelity, and adopted ethics. Being honest, in this context, is about openness, notwithstanding the obligations of sensible commercial and political confidentiality. It will mean making concessions to good argument when these should prevail for the wider interest and it will mean avoiding the sins of selective or convenient omission simply to win an argument. Fidelity in legal and financial matters is not only essential for a director; it is also a powerful weapon in establishing a personal reputation. Nothing impresses staff more than when they see members of the board make personal telephone calls from their own cell-phones or post their personal mail with stamps from their own wallets and purses. Fidelity is one of the few absolutes in corporate affairs. Indiscretions, however small, will tarnish reputations for ever. Ethical values are what drive people to do the right things for the right reasons. Continuously ethical behaviour is a key component in building trust and it is a hard but rewarding taskmaster. When directors are admired for their integrity they invite others to share issues and concerns without fear. This can be critical when mitigating the risks of decision making.

Judgement is the fourth, and most important, vehicle for adding value. Without good judgement, all else is ephemeral. Given good leadership from the boardroom, blessed with objectivity in its deliberations and integrity in its motives, it is the application of sound judgement that delivers ultimate value. The key to sound judgement is often one of balance. Reconciling the head (ie the quantifiable aspects of knowledge, skills, and intellect) with the heart (ie the qualitative aspects of culture, effort, and emotion) is generally the secret. It is quite normal for directors to disagree about the best way forward. However, conceding an important point against one's better judgement can be unusually disconcerting. Everyone can make mistakes from time to time and they must be allowed to do so in the cause of building experience but when the poor judgement of others is backed by insufficient resolve it is likely to lead to embarrassing exposure.

The Roles

Directors play a number of different roles in the boardroom and these roles provide opportunities to add value.

As a trustee, the director acts to serve the interests of the stakeholders by ensuring that the organisation is well positioned at all times to adapt itself to new and evolving circumstances. A trustee is directly responsible for protecting value and ensuring that new value created is fairly attributed to all beneficiaries.

As an ambassador, the director represents the organisation and its interests in the outside world. In this role the director needs to present a positive image which objectively reflects the stature of the organisation. Playing this role will fall mostly to chairmen but in their absence other board members will be expected to fill the vacuum. Good ambassadors can win surprising advantage from neutral and uncommitted situations.

As a networker, the director provides the enterprise with a growing resource of contacts and influence for business development. This role is central to the identification and creation of new opportunities for revenue growth, without which all organisations eventually stagnate and atrophy. When directors speak, listeners will assume they are speaking for their organisation. This gives great power, and responsibility, to the networker when they act as principals in building new revenue earning opportunities.

As a catalyst, the director energises boardroom colleagues for new challenges. However, from time to time a catalyst will also be needed to reconcile entrenched and opposing views around the board. This role is often undervalued and frequently absent. Catalysts are proactive and prompted by the desire to ensure that others use their talent for the greater benefit of the organisation.

As a role model, the director can personify the aspirations and ambitions of younger people in the organisation. In the way that leaders have followers, so are role models adopted by admirers in ways that may never become explicit. Role models emerge when some aspect of outstanding performance or achievement becomes widely known. By behaving in ways that others will copy in developing their own careers or interests the role model exerts great influence. A good role model will pass on experience freely, perpetuate all that is good about an organisation, underpin the prevailing culture, and build a platform for continuity. However, occasionally strong role models can be major barriers to essential change if they support the traditional over the necessary and these will need to be won over when dramatic changes are needed.

As a professional manager, the director can ensure that sound business practices and processes are adopted and followed by an organisation. This professionalism and the experience behind it should be a key component in the elimination of waste and the mitigation of risks and uncertainties. Often, insights from one functional area about another can make significant differences in performance.

Playing out the various roles as a director will project a sense of style. Directors, as a group, will implicitly or explicitly set the style in their organisation. If that style is consistent with the values and the culture of the enterprise, harmony will result. If not, it will lead to confusion and possible demoralisation. While style is an important attribute for a director it should not be confused with or substituted for substance.

The Obligations

Directors are usually appointed for their experience, which could come from inside or outside the organisation. They therefore have an obligation to ensure that their experience is both matched to and relevant for the needs of the enterprise. Additionally, there will be some key behavioural obligations to be recognised if added value is to be delivered. Directors need to be serious and responsible but not aloof. An open-door policy to offer easy access at well advertised times will achieve this.

Professional obligations are important, too. Directors should apply their own brand of intellectual rigour and emotional understanding to situations at all times. This is the foundation for offering wisdom and pragmatism. Whereas experience has its roots in the past, wisdom comes from an ability to anticipate the impact of events on the future. The ability to avoid major surprises and to navigate situations advantageously will deliver possibly the greatest degree of added value that a director may contribute.

A Critical Perspective

The boardroom is essentially a strategic forum. It is not the place to re-run tactical and operational decisions. Having a true strategic perspective is one of the biggest challenges facing a new director but his perspective is central to the concept of added value in the boardroom. In quoted companies, the pressures of half-yearly reporting invite constant concern about operational issues and it will take a degree of strong leadership by the chairman to ensure that strategic considerations are not only recognised but given priority.

The Metrics

Added value can only be demonstrated through measurement. There is an old adage that says if something cannot be measured, it cannot be controlled. Measurement can be very difficult, especially when qualitative issues, such as quality and service, dominate considerations.

Statutory measures come in the form of statements about assets, profits, and cash flows. These statements are merely records of what has happened and presented in a standardised reporting format. They are not basic instruments for control. The balance sheet does, however, record value and its movement from previous statements. In contrast, the profit and loss account merely records an agreed profit for the purposes of assessing taxation liabilities. Many organisations that have attempted to control activities through monthly profit and loss accounts have been known to fail as they get overtaken by cash flow problems. Something with more utility is needed to analyse added value and its attribution to activities and contributions.

The traditional definition of added value at a corporate level is revenue *less* purchases. This definition places all administrative costs in *added value* whether or not these activities are efficient. If administrative costs are reduced, and all else remains the same then the added value does not change but profits certainly do and to greater advantage. In other words, added value is equivalent to profits *plus* added costs. Simply maximising added value on the basis of this simple definition can produce bizarre, unexpected and undesirable results.

There is now a growing tendency to define added value in terms of two independent but complementary components. The first component is economic added value (EVA) which measures what is added to purchases through the use of productive resources and the deployment of skilled labour. The second component is market added value (MVA) which measures the premium over strict producer cost that the market will bear to pay for distribution, quality and service. These parameters are much more useful to work with as EVA can be optimised while MVA can be maximised without conflict. It is usually a salutary exercise for directors to establish and quantify what contributions to EVA and MVA can be attributed unambiguously to the activities of the board.

Added value concepts are often confused with productivity issues. Greater productivity is always valuable and is something that should be pursued relentlessly. It can be measured in a variety of ways, ranging from the simple sales value per employee to the ratio of standard hour of product delivered to actual hours paid for. Productivity measures have extra utility when used as part of a benchmarking exercise which compares results across companies, markets, or products.

The Kipling "If…" Test

Professionalism is inextricably tied to adding value. Directors should have commitments to getting things right-first-time (RFT), to continuous professional development (CPD), and to ethical behaviour at all times.

So, what does it take to be a credible and successful director? Kipling gives a clue in his celebrated work "If…". This can be parodied, with suitable apologies, as follows.

If you can form your own views without being influenced by the mere status of others,

If you can create alliances from disparate groups and hold them together in a worthy common cause,

If you can manage your own behaviour so as never to offend when you are probably right,

And,

If you know when to resign for the greater good of the enterprise,

Then, you will be a director, my friend.

Behavioural Barriers

Behavioural barriers can be the biggest challenge to becoming an effective member of the board. It has been said that we are all prisoners of our childhood and the experiences we had then. Living in the present may need a conscious break with the past. The challenge is to see the present for what it is and not allow it to be distorted by memories. Three, not untypical examples, will serve to make the point.

A managing director of a FTSE 250 company had experienced great trauma in his childhood when his parents' relationship broke down. They separated and subsequently divorced. During this period he had taken on the role of holding the warring factions together and developed some finely honed interpersonal skills in his attempts to be the peacemaker. In his corporate leadership role he found it hard to live with the natural tensions between powerful personalities around the top table. With his innate fear of conflict, he saw the hard-talking confrontational style around the boardroom as negative and threatening whereas in this instance it was a sign of vigorous health and a source of effective decision making.

The finance director of a leading property company had been the first in her family to go to university and had qualified brilliantly. This should have been a very positive aspect of her life but this was not the case. As with many individuals with a similar background, she felt fearful of outshining one or both of her parents when she was growing up. Her parents had not had the good fortune to go to university or even secure a decent education. Her fears constantly undermined her own performance. This syndrome, commonly known as *envy pre-emption* describes the case when an individual fears another person's envy, real or imagined, and consequently reduces their own capacity to perform to avoid having to deal with it. A mentoring programme explored these fears and established they were just that – fears. Her parents had been delighted with her achievements and the blockage was removed.

A chairman of a traditional organisation had purposely appointed a "new style" CEO to shake up his company and move it forward. He was then surprised when the abrasive Antipodean started to rub people up the wrong way. Moreover, the CEO could not understand when the chairman told him that he was often seen as cold and hostile by others. The HR manager took it upon herself to get the CEO to modify his behaviour. It turned out that the issues were rooted in the loss of his father in early life. He had spent his entire working life attempting to prove his worth to the father he never had during the critical years of his upbringing. This had resulted in tremendous personal drive but came at the cost of bruising behaviour. He needed to find a new way to validate his performance and recognise that he was capable of doing a good job. This relieved the pressures he had placed on others.

Not all behavioural issues come from childhood. Acquired behavioural characteristics can pose an equal threat. A classic transitional problem was experienced by an executive of a FTSE 100 company with its origins in the public sector. The executive had made a great success of running operations in North America and was highly regarded by the board of the company. The company had a distinctive macho-management style and the executive, on his return to join the board, felt very much out of his comfort zone in his new situation. His response was to talk, almost incessantly, in an effort to impress his new colleagues. He made no impact, other than annoying everyone, and by talking and not listening or thinking his technical performance suffered too.

Behaviour acquired by working in one sort of culture can be debilitating when circumstances change. This happened to some long-serving, and successful, directors when they suddenly found themselves exposed in uncomfortable positions when ownership changes forced a change of chairman. A major retailer had grown to be a dominant regional force from its origins as a family company. Part of its success had been the way it had retained and translated its values in serving customers as it had grown. The first chairman of the company when it went public, a member of the original family owners, was a gifted and charismatic personality and the new company prospered under his leadership, developing a national presence. When the chairman retired, and some new non-executive board appointments were made, the long-serving executive directors became increasingly detached, disillusioned and ineffective. They had grown in their positions with a clear and authoritative leader on hand and this support had now gone leaving a vacuum in strategic direction. They all struggled to understand their roles in relation to their executive tasks and were quite unable to make the sort of contributions to the business that is expected of senior executives. It took some time, and some deep mentoring programmes, for these long-serving directors to grow into their new situation and shed their dependence on the previous chairman.

Occasionally, a group behavioural phenomenon will emerge. During the wave of privatisation projects, when nationalised industries were being broken up and the parts were being spun-off, in one case a new company was formed to take over some of the heavy repair and maintenance facilities of the old corporation. The facilities were modern and comprehensive. The workshops involved had developed an outstanding reputation for the quality of their work within both the public sector and the commercial sector of their market. The new investors were keen for some of the managers to be motivated through a series of appointments to the board of the new company. These managers, who were competent at a trade skills level, never understood their new roles and responsibilities and rather resented the presence of the new investors despite being awarded significant amounts of stock in the new venture. The recently elevated former managers hi-jacked the board meetings to pursue their own personal gripes about the relative awards of stock and completely neglected the needs of the business. As the workload ran down with the disappearance of the former nationalised corporation the company went into a spiral of decline and went bankrupt. It was a sad end to a fine facility.

5

How the Board Works

In the UK, at the time of writing, the regulation of business and corporate practices is the responsibility of the Department for Business Innovation and Skills (BIS). Compliance is enforced through the courts. Historically, regulation has been vested in various predecessors of BIS, principally the Department of Trade (DoT) and the Department of Trade and Industry (DTI) and their respective initials can be found in many documents and references.

The Rules

Legislation affecting the management of businesses and their related corporate entities is enshrined in various Company Acts. The principal objectives of these acts are twofold. Firstly, to provide a framework of protection for those parties most at risk from corporate activities. These will be, typically, creditors, investors, and employees. Secondly, the acts set out key responsibilities for company directors with particular regard for corporate solvency and the fidelity of their behaviour.

The success of companies as a suitable vehicle for business can be traced to two pieces of enlightened development. The emergence and growing sophistication of the joint-stock company during the eighteenth century provided a popular and efficient vehicle to accept investment funds for new ventures. With the contemporaneous development of a stock exchange, which provided readily accessible liquidity, the foundations were laid for modern capitalism. The introduction of limited liability protection concepts for ordinary shareholders during the nineteenth century gave added impetus to the expansion of the corporate sector of the economy. Subsequent legislation, that now comprises the Company Acts, has usually been driven by responses to events that have exposed creditors, investors and employees to abuses in the exercise of power by companies or their directors.

BIS today has the powers to investigate any aspect of company activities at any time. It can investigate issues of fraud or embezzlement and it will have the support of the Serious Fraud Office (SFO), if necessary, to do so. It can pursue the best interests of the public in proposals for corporate acquisitions and can investigate specific cases through referrals to the Monopolies and Mergers Commission (MMC) and it can support the best interests of the public in maintaining fair competition and fair pricing practices by referrals to the Office of Fair Trading (OFT). In discharging these duties BIS will inevitably play a role with a very high profile and often make national news. However, BIS also plays an important part in the elimination of bad practices in business and corporate affairs.

For many years, if a company wanted access to capital through public subscription the rules for raising that money were set by the London Stock Exchange (LSE). Today, these rules, and their associated codes of practice to be followed by corporate management, are enforced by the Financial Services Authority (FSA). The rules cover issues such as the conventions to be adopted for reporting to shareholders; the procedures for dealing with price sensitive information; the curbs on the use of insider information; the procedures for and obligations in making take-over bids for quoted companies; and the constraints on the share dealings of directors. Much of this is directed at maintaining fairness for small investors when buying and selling shares.

Additionally, the LSE rules encouraged management to adopt various practices deemed to be good for the corporate governance of publicly-quoted companies. As referred to in Chapter 2, compliance with statutory codes of practice for good corporate governance has become a growing feature of life in the boardroom, and a summary of the main provisions of the Combined Code is set out in Appendix 2. Indeed, compliance has become such a big issue that a newly appointed director may well conclude that it represents not only the biggest new challenge but possibly the only new challenge to face in the boardroom.

The Practices

The effectiveness of a board will be heavily influenced by the capabilities of the chairman and the quality of the agenda and its supporting papers. The agenda should be composed by the chairman, in consultation with the CEO, having due regard for both long-term and current issues facing the company. A proper agenda will be supported by the minutes of previous meetings for review, a series of management reports relating to performance, and papers with proposals for specific decisions or change. These papers should be circulated well in advance of the board meeting by the company secretary or the chairman's secretary.

The minutes of past meetings should be a clear record of decisions taken, the essence of any important discussions with the respective conclusions, and the assignment of tasks for action and follow-up. The drafting of minutes often leaves a lot to be desired. Some chairmen prefer a minimalist approach to their publication. In these instances, no discussions may be recorded (often, on the grounds that this may indicate less than unanimity or embarrassing uncertainty) and only the decisions taken are referred to. In contrast, the minutes of public-sector bodies are often masterpieces of prose whereby all points of discussion are faithfully recorded (usually at the contributor's behest) but conclusions may be entirely absent and decisions taken (if any) will appear to emerge by consensus and be rarely attributable to someone that may be challenged in the future by later scrutiny. These models of obfuscation now approach the status of an art form!

Report papers are likely to follow an agreed or stand-ardised format that will have evolved with experience over the years to ensure that their content is relevant, unambiguous, and readily understood. Much work often goes into the preparation of such reports and when they are tabled the author or owner often seeks to consume time at the board meeting commensurate with the effort put into its preparation. There is a good case for maintaining that a standing report of this kind should not be examined in painstaking detail unless there is something unusual in its content. If performances are to budget then it only takes a sentence to say so and move on. Performance reports can provide endless fascination for executive directors as they alternately project their own importance and criticise the efforts of their colleagues. It is the chairman's responsibility to ensure that the deliberations of the Executive Committee (which is the proper forum for these sorts of discussion) do not intrude into the boardroom.

Papers with proposals for change are most important. A good paper will comprise the background or context of the proposal, the proposition itself with some clear arguments for and against the proposition for objective discussion, and an unambiguous statement of sponsorship or support. These papers should be the very essence of a board meeting but are rarely prepared with the care they deserve. This often reflects pressures of work or the urgency of some changes. A good chairman will insist on a minimum standard of quality and presentation for these papers and should be so intimately familiar with their content as to introduce the item on the agenda in a way that demonstrates a truly masterful understanding. Whenever such papers are put forward to the board for rubber-stamping it is a sign that the board has long abdicated its responsibilities or that it has become the poodle of the chairman or the CEO.

In managing the deliberations of the board, a good chairman will ensure that discussions are open and constructive, that every member is drawn in to give a perspective, and that discussions are brought to a conclusion, as opposed to being concluded. Summarising discussions and drawing appropriate conclusions are critical responsibilities of the chairman. The conclusions, however, may not command unanimous support or may be challenged on philosophical grounds. On these occasions it will be sensible to take a vote. Voting may also be required when a decision is called for so as to establish positions or give legitimacy to planned actions. Some chairmen, erroneously, regard a vote as a failure on their part to win an argument and will resist calls for a vote. Voting is a healthy sign and is useful in emphasising the responsibilities of the directors when major decisions are needed.

As the CEO, and other executive directors, will have to take operational decisions out of expediency without an opportunity to refer issues immediately to the board, where ultimate authority may lie, there has to be a pragmatic solution to reconcile these realities. Most companies operate, often tacitly, a form of advise-and-consent practice. Decisions are taken by executives committed to advising the board at the earliest opportunity for confirmation on the basis that they sincerely expect to win the consent of the board. When consent is not forthcoming, for whatever reason, the issue becomes one of resignation for some party.

Some Critical Reservations

Boards are just as prone to make mistakes as flawed individuals are and a board can be particularly exposed when it comes to people-related issues.

Mergers and acquisitions present very distinctive problems. A clash of cultures, temperament, and style is quite usual and difficult to plan for. Sometimes the best of motives, too, can come seriously adrift. Following a complicated and protracted series of acquisitions in the computer software business by an American venture capital company, there was a need to appoint a new CEO to run the new entity from a London base. Remarkably, no plans had been made for the leadership of the company during the investment process. A board was formed from people drawn from the leading components of the new company and this board was invited to pick one of their number as CEO. The person selected turned out to be a complete rascal and presided over a period when corruption grew to rampant proportions. It took some time for the shareholders to recognise the corruption and even more time to correct the situation. The company, which started with outstanding prospects, became badly damaged and still struggles to compete through its losses in profitability and market development time despite the quality of its intellectual property.

Taking the easy way out on people-related issues invariably fails but the prospect of a clever *finesse* can still deceive. Some boardroom appointments are made, initially for a quieter life, but all too predictably they dissolve into the complete opposite and turn into a great mistake. An international engineering company had its domestic division run by a very powerful personality who was not a technical specialist. The division made good profits but this was mostly a result of selling very sharp low-risk contracts that were not at all client-friendly. Slowly, the good reputation of the company was being adulterated as clients stopped coming back with new bidding offers, but the profits picture was camouflaging the real situation. This domestic CEO lobbied very hard for a position on the main board, and despite his general unpopularity and the low opinion of his understanding of engineering risk, he was eventually appointed. Then the real problems began. There were soon major divisions on the board as it split into two warring factions. One faction was principally the group of engineering specialists who were rightly concerned about risk, reputation, and contractual transparency; the other group was principally the non-executive directors who thought they were supporting what the City institutions were looking for. More and more contracts were taken on where the engineering risk had been ignored or dismissed and profits started to evaporate. However, it was only when some close acolytes of the former domestic CEO were jailed for serious malpractice that the board found the courage to part company with their colleague. Within two years the company went into terminal decline.

Boards must maintain the talent base of the organisation for which it is responsible. No regimental officer would fall into the trap of not securing a proper succession within the regiment to perpetuate its values and traditions. In business, especially today, genuine talent is very valuable and highly mobile. A newly appointed CEO of a major hotel chain arrived as a newcomer to the business. Fortunately, instead of introducing a rash of new initiatives to signal his presence, for his first three months the CEO disappeared into the belly of the organisation on a quest to understand the company's core issues. The business was regarded as solid and dependable if a little fuddy-duddy. The company had a major problem retaining its young talent. Although its three year training programme attracted top talent at a graduate level the best tended to leave within two years of completing the programme. The more dynamic young people simply could not see any opportunities for career progression and took their chances elsewhere, leaving the weaker candidates behind to clog the spaces immediately below board level. The CEO's investment in understanding his new role allowed him to reflect properly on the problems of the company and he successfully introduced a junior board to mirror the activities of the main board. This brought a new lease of life to the organisation.

The evolution and development of corporate government practices, since the Cadbury Report in 1992, has given new impetus to the roles of non-executive directors on the boards of companies. It is now all but mandatory for companies to set up permanent committees of the board to deal with compliance, audit, executive compensation, and nominations for board appointments, and these are now regarded as essential for good governance. The independence of these committees through the appointment of suitable non-executive directors was enshrined in the Higgs Report in 2003. However, the collective performance of the resulting group of non-executive directors since the Higgs Report has, at best, been disappointing. Far too many powerful CEOs and chairmen have not been adequately challenged by their non-executive directors and the recent failures at The Royal Bank of Scotland and Northern Rock have further dented their standing. Despite the best intentions of the Higgs Report, non-executives have become part of a far too cosy club where reciprocal offers are legion between the executives of one company and those of another, whereby they indulge in cross-appointments for non-executive roles. Currently (November 2009), the Walker enquiry is expected to address some of these disappointments coupled with some commentary on the role shareholders should play in holding boards to account.

The case for greater shareholder assertion has no firmer foundation than the recent controversy over bankers' bonuses. Following the bail-out of some retail banks and their *de facto* nationalisation, it is remarkable to see some fundamentally-flawed management practices being perpetuated. The compensation of the CEO of a bank which is either a public company or a publicly-owned company does not warrant its being set at a level which can only be justified if the assets were personally owned and put at risk by the CEO. A CEO is only a superintendent of the assets owned by shareholders and should be compensated accordingly. While great shareholder benefits will come from a steady growth in, say earning per share, and a growing share price, the proper way for a CEO to benefit from this is to make a personal investment and coincidentally show commitment. Highly geared bonus payments and free stock awards are not appropriate arrangements outside genuine partnerships.

6

Key Skills for Directors

As executives make progress in an organisation, their use of time will change in ways that will reflect their increasing experience, responsibilities, and authority. This evolution and its implied pattern of career development are illustrated in outline in Figure 6.1. The reader should test where they are on the diagram by simply examining the indicated deployment of activity suggested for their age. Major differences between the reader's actual use of time and that indicated by the diagram should prompt some compelling questions about the difference. Whilst the diagram is not definitive, differences in time (age) or the balance of activities may give insights into career development or specialisation bias respectively.

Strategic Skills

Strategy is the positioning of resources, in anticipation of threats or prospective opportunities, to secure increased competitive advantage. Success then comes from effective implementation. In contrast, tactics involve the immediate engagement of available resources so as to win current or localised advantage. Strategic issues are boardroom affairs whilst tactical manoeuvring should be the exclusive concern of executives.

Figure 6.1 Profile of Time Demands During Career.

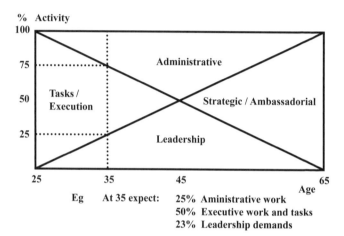

The strategic skill-set is very different from that demanded of senior people in an executive role. Concepts are more relevant than detail. For very pressed executives the thought of spending time in a reflective way may seem both irresponsible and very unsatisfying. For some it will even take on frightening dimensions in the absence of familiar boundaries values.

Business strategy is driven essentially by some evolving vision about the future. It will encompass new product-market opportunities, the exploitation of innovation and research, and the pursuit of a distinctive set of values. It will involve the development of key resources and the disposal of marginal assets; it may open up new partnerships and alliances; and it will demand the identification of new risks and their cost-effective mitigation. Strategy will be heavily influenced by external events and factors outside the control of the business. As with many endeavours, timing is likely to be a critical factor in the pursuit of success.

Some stratagems can be universal. It is never disadvantageous to be the least-cost producer in a healthy or growing market. This position will provide the greatest opportunity for profit and the greatest degree of protection against competition. Again, it will always be worth directing a significant part of a research budget to find ways of making one's current business redundant, on the grounds that if it is at all possible it would be better to discover this ahead of a competitor.

In contrast, there are some stratagems that are regarded as universal but are, on examination, found to be fatally flawed. Outsourcing in pursuit of becoming the least-cost supplier will provide only temporary advantage or respite unless it is part of a programme to re-insource at a later date on the back of new or next generation technology. Continuously outsourcing to stay competitive will continuously reduce economic added value to vanishing point, whilst the maintenance of market added value may mask this decline for some time. This stratagem turns all manufacturing companies into trading companies in due course with the ultimate consequence of putting all manufacturing into stone-age Papua New Guinea where labour costs will be rock-bottom! It also postpones the drive to find new sources of productivity.

At first sight the differences between a least-cost producer strategy and a least-cost supplier strategy may appear to be too subtle to be significant. Yet one will offer growing success, albeit with considerable effort, and the other will offer only slow decline, albeit with some comfort for those except the last.

Strategy needs an evolving vision as a primer. This makes it a divergent process in that possibilities grow with time and programmes may never be completed in a conventional sense. In fact, at any one time an organisation needs to have a number of strategic options open so that it can accommodate unpredictable events and opportunities. Too many companies see strategy as a convergent process that focuses on some arbitrary point in time for completion. This approach will close down options as time moves forward as opposed to removing only invalid options for the future. Living with divergent phenomena encapsulates the need for a strategic mindset.

Decision Making

Decision making is a process that encompasses the assembly of facts, their objective analysis, the drawing of conclusions, and the commitment to action. Decisiveness is central to leadership but decisions must be sound and then applied to make any sort of progress.

The effective use of facts is governed by the rules of evidence and proof. This is of great importance today as data are easily found in overwhelming volumes through internet sources. Facts need direct and credible attribution to be of value. Hearsay, which frequently masquerades as evidence, may be interesting but will usually be misleading. The objective of fact-finding is to form helpful conclusions about the best way forward. Facts come with different degrees of power. Qualitative information from credible sources would be at one end of the scale and quantitative information would be at the other end. If propositions can be proved they become facts and very powerful ones too.

Science has contributed a number of methods to build proof. Firstly, there is *reductio ad absurdum*. By making a proposition then showing that it implies impossible results the proposition can be disproved. Proving that prime numbers form an infinite series was established this way when the assumption that they were finite led to absurd results. Sometimes it is possible to formulate a solution to a problem without a clear understanding as to why it works. This is empirical proof and is very powerful in science. The relationship between money supply and inflation is based on empirical evidence. When some things are known to be true, it may be possible to demonstrate that other things may be true as a consequence. This is proof by induction. Euclidean geometry largely comes into this category. Occasionally, some phenomena can be proved analytically and shown to be universal truths. This is extremely powerful when possible and a good example would be the celebrated theorem of Pythagoras regarding right angled triangles. Most proof is best described as experimental and reflects the standard scientific method. When observations are made the rational person will look for a pattern and attempt to explain the observations in quantitative terms. This explanation or theory is then used to predict what might happen under different conditions. If these new conditions can be replicated the prediction can be tested by observation. If the prediction is valid the theory might be relevant. Continual testing for different conditions with successful outcomes will lend growing credibility to the theory. Without the disciplines of proof, people are reduced to believing that what is right is a function of the stature of the person who makes the proposition. As the Pope was more important than Galileo the western world resisted the thought that the earth orbited the sun.

Analysis is the responsibility of management. Facts are enhanced by analysis and as a consequence may come to be regarded as proprietary or commercially sensitive. However, it is the ability to draw valid conclusions that is the key to effective decision making. This is both the responsibility and the hallmark of leaders. Conclusions, when drawn, must owned by leaders and command their total commitment. When Margaret Thatcher was Prime Minister she was convinced that inflation would come under control with new restrictions on money supply. The proof she had gave her conviction and she carried it through to success despite the doubts of others who were unable to accept the proposition. This is the point where added value is delivered with the greatest leverage.

Action is always the consequence of agreed compromise. The compromise should reflect the realities of implementation (such as budgetary limitations) without in any way diluting the essence or principles behind a conclusion. Implementation should be delegated to convinced executives.

Reviews are an essential management discipline. Few decisions are ever entirely clear-cut and mistakes need early detection and correction. Few decisions also remain unaffected by events and without the disciplines of review it will become impossible to effect justified change as events unfold.

Decision making as a skill requires objectivity, a freedom from vested interests, the application of rigour in analyses, and the exercise of sound judgement.

Effective decision making requires, in addition, a sensitivity to circumstances, the willingness to shoulder responsibility, and the courage to act.

Advocacy

Advocacy is the art of effective communication in support of a proposition. It is a critical instrument of leadership. It has no boundaries and, when successful, it allows ordinary people to achieve extraordinary results. It has distinctive structural components which could qualify it as a science but it also has the performance dynamics that confirm it as an art.

Successful advocacy is founded on the concept of a thesis which encapsulates critical conclusions in the form of a proposition. A thesis sentence may appear to be an abstract concept but it can often double, in a shortened form, as a title or branding statement for the issue or situation under review. No effective communication is possible without a thesis sentence.

Consider the following proposition. When infrastructure is funded by the private sector, the demands on debt finance will be so great that it will become essential to secure contracted lines of income in advance, and that the engineering involved be based on least-cost practices, even at the expense of user-friendly features. This is a good example of a thesis sentence. It explains why, for example, the Eurotunnel project was a drive on–drive off railway service. This was the least-cost solution. It also explains why the project has struggled commercially despite its engineering success. The company failed to secure any contracted lines of income. These could only have come from British Rail

(BR) and its French equivalent, SNCF. However, the British government took the view that a contract from BR to use the facility would amount to a government guarantee for the project in another form and it was not prepared to grant this.

A successful manager must master the arts of persuasion and advocacy to become an effective director. A newly appointed marketing director, aged 36, could not understand why his early contributions at board meetings had not been well-received by his colleagues. He had been a successful manager within the company for some time and was unused to a lacklustre response from colleagues. He had taken time to prepare for his first board meeting recognising the importance of making a good impression. He soon realised that by taking his command and control tactics into the boardroom he was going to make his approach jar. His insistence on closing down options, removing uncertainty, and reaching conclusions quickly ran counter to what was expected of him in his new role. The chairman would repeatedly interrupt his meticulously planned presentations with: "No, no, no. Don't rush to a conclusion. All we want you to do is to put forward your position on the issue. Let others probe and challenge your thinking." What was important to the board was that by a process of constructive challenge and debate it would eventually attain a collective view of the best way forward.

The most successful messaging formats are based on courtroom practices and broadcasting models. When these are applied to speeches, presentations, reports, or videos, the formats are a variation on the same theme. The courtroom model is set out in Appendix 3 and the broadcasting model in Appendix 4. These models need to be learned and practised by all leaders. The courtroom model is more appropriate for formal situations and the broadcasting model is more useful in informal circumstances or where time is very limited.

Successful advocacy is aided when a proper selection of media options is made. With the proliferation of communications technology this selection process can appear to be a daunting prospect. Speeches should be used to put forward an opinion or to state a position in an attempt to persuade. They should be concise and rarely justify more than five minutes. Presentations should be used to convince a targeted audience about a course of action. They will benefit from using visual aids if audience interest is to be maintained. If the content is substantially verbal, interest will wane after ten minutes; if the content is substantially visual the presentation can run for up to 20 minutes. Reports, in documentary form, are best used to support a course of action and act as a source of future reference. They should be as concise as possible and be capable of being studied and understood by a competent or qualified reader within an hour. Debates may comprise a mix of speeches, presentations and reports. All debates benefit from using a formal structure such as that to be found in the Oxford Union. In a boardroom context this formality should be more implicit than explicit. All debate must be drawn to a conclusion, if it is to deliver any value, and the summing up should be undertaken by the chairman in no more than five minutes.

All advocacy is a performance and, as such, it will benefit from some degree of stage management. Care should be taken in choosing venues, adapting the layout of facilities for good effect, and using the most appropriate (and reliable) equipment. The watchword is the simpler the props the better. Presenters need to be in control of their audiences and have a clear procedure in place to answer any questions. Poor stage management signals incompetence. Good stage management will help the audience better understand the proposition and the reasoning behind it. Slickness is unwelcome outside pure entertainment.

The key skills for advocacy includes the ability to construct a thesis sentence, mastery of the language, familiarity with the rules of evidence, and an understanding of proof based on the scientific method.

Enquiry

Enquiry is the art of unearthing evidence. It is helped by a natural curiosity. It plays a critical role in keeping leaders in touch with their organisation and its constituencies. Good enquiry is the basis of insight.

Enquiry should start with an anti-thesis proposition. These are devices to draw counter arguments that will help in establishing otherwise obscure underlying realities. Consider the following proposition. If the company were to eliminate its partner in distribution operations by taking the whole activity in-house, it could pass on the savings to customers and become more price competitive. This proposition, as an anti-thesis, should draw someone to observe, possibly, that such a move would require new investment and that the in-house operations would no longer benefit from the economies of scale on offer from the company's partner. This is the essence of enquiry.

A technique for drawing people to reveal their positions or understanding of an issue involves the use of open and closed questions in a structured way. Open questions will allow respondents to set the scope of their answers. Any extra emphasis placed on issues in reply will usually reveal underlying opinions or values. Consider the following question. What has caused our liquidity crisis in extending new credit lines to our customers? This is an open question. The respondent at this point is free to offer any explanation. The response might be that borrowers in the sub-prime market have been defaulting on an unexpected scale and have exposed the capital adequacy of the company. Closed questions are more highly directed and should have much simpler answers although this should not be confused with the answers being easier to find. The original questioner, in the situation above, may now consider asking whether this will mean that the company is faced with writing-off a new tranche of bad debt with immediate effect. This is a closed question where the answer will be a yes or a no. All enquiry should be brought to a conclusion through the use of appropriate closed questions.

Enquiry is more effective when it is undertaken in an unthreatening way. Terry Brown was a senior policeman intimately involved in the introduction of tape recorders and cameras when evidence was being taken from suspects and witnesses in criminal enquiries. In his view this move changed the nature of the enquiry process in many unexpected and beneficial ways. Most importantly, the purpose of questioning switched from getting a confession to establishing what happened. After all, when events have been established it is for a jury to decide on guilt. The less threatening approach that was forced by the presence of recording equipment, and a subtle change in objectives, transformed the pursuit of justice. The choice of time and place in creating the right conditions for effective enquiry is usually critical to its success. However, few people put the proper time and effort into getting it right. Indeed, many people like to ask questions in a casual or unstructured environment in the hope that the respondent may be caught off-guard.

Enquiry is often aided when people work as a team. Respondents often attempt to "second guess" a line of questioning. This may be done either to obscure some sensitive issue or to give the questioner what the respondent feels they may want. A team approach can demand greater attention by a respondent giving them less time to think beyond the questions alone. Rapid changes in the direction of questioning by having two parallel agendas with two different questioners often leaves a respondent with no option but call things the way they are.

7

Are You Ready?

Test Yourself

The following are a series of test questions which simply have the answers *yes* or *no*. These will not, however, be simple questions and few of the answers may be proved categorically to be the right one or the wrong one. This is part of the challenge and attraction of being a director in a boardroom environment. The suggested answers and the scoring system immediately follows the next section together with some comments as to the intent of the questions.

The Questions

1. Are you prepared to resign at a moment's notice without compensation if you disagree fundamentally with board policy?

2. Would you accept responsibility, with your colleagues, for any consequential impact of the activities of your organisation?

3. Would you trust your colleagues totally and implicitly in terms of their fidelity, judgement, and political motivation?

4. If you are not a finance specialist, would you be prepared to disagree with the Finance Director over the Annual Report and Accounts if you felt that, say, contingent liabilities had not been properly evaluated, exposed, and provided for?

5. Would you be prepared to withdraw, gracefully, an application for a particular capital expenditure that you have sponsored, if the collective view of your boardroom colleagues is that other programmes, at this time, should get priority?

6. Would you feel a responsibility to investigate charges levelled by environmentalists that your organisation is, say, causing neighbourhood distress through its night time delivery activities?

7. Would you be prepared to turn down work if you felt that your ability, as an organisation, to deliver a proper service was not up to your standards of performance in other areas?

8. Would you be prepared to set aside your concerns about an issue if you were encouraged to do so by the Chairman in the cause of wider board harmony?

9. Would you throw your weight behind a proposal where your natural position is neutral-to-unfavourably disposed if in doing so you could secure support for another of your own favoured proposals?

10. Can you identify the context of your likely responsibilities on the board in terms of the organisation and its prevailing culture?

11 Are you comfortable with your likely role, its implied commitment, and the type of contribution it is likely to demand from you?

12. Could you justify why profitability might always prevail as a measure over social or environmental issues within a business?

13. Could you reconcile a lifestyle on business expenses which you choose not to maintain in your private life?

14. Would you know from where you might draw your greatest support in the boardroom and would you know where your positions might be more actively challenged?

15. Do you always attempt to establish how different parties might vote on issues before coming to your own conclusions or before being tested on your views?

16. Do you consider a position on the board to be, mostly, a recognition of good service by a respected senior executive?

17. Should the roles of chairman and chief executive be combined when an outstanding single leader emerges or when there is an absence of even an adequate candidate for one of the positions?

18. If a business is dominated by one particular division or function, should the head of that entity have an automatic right of appointment to the board?

19. Is profitability more of a measure of business success than a long track record for successful product development?

20. Do you believe that people perform better under close supervision and direction rather that when they are left alone to work within a looser framework?

21. Do you subscribe to the view that "all is fair in love, war, and business, provided it is legal" in getting your own views to prevail?

22. When you are the most senior person in a group charged with making a decision, do you prefer to put forward your views first?

23. Would you run your accounts payable to 120 days-of-sales if you could prevail on your suppliers to agree?

24. Do you believe that environmental problems are the sole responsibility of the community and not that of the businessman?

25. Do you believe that taxation should be the primary mechanism for funding public infra-structure programmes?

26. Are you comfortable with the notion that professionals may enjoy privileges that non-professionals may be denied?

27. Could you identify the areas where you might add value to your organisation through the membership of your board?

28. Do you have a vision for your organisation which you like to share with others at every opportunity to do so?

29. Do you believe in the tenet "If it isn't broke, don't fix it"?

30. Are you prepared to change your position in the light of new evidence or a more compelling argument?

31. Are you prepared to spend time again as a pupil to become more proficient in new business practices or skills outside your own field of experience?

32. Are you able to establish, independently, the liquidity position of your organisation and, hence, its solvency?

33. Do you know how price sensitive announcements should be made to the public?

34. Do you know what should happen if your company plans to acquire stock in another public company that will take its holding to over 29%?

35. Do you see board meetings as rubber-stamping exercises to give authority to operational decisions that have already been taken?

36. Do you prefer to signal your positions on key issues without prior notice at meetings on the grounds that this will produce a more spontaneous discussion and less political posturing?

37. Do you believe that boards should probably always seek a consensus, which the chairman can easily articulate, rather than resort to voting, which might prove divisive?

The Answers and their Scores

The answers offered are the ones preferred by the authors. They may have other merits, too. For the preferred answer three points may be awarded, but for the alternative only one point may be scored.

Question	Score		Comments
	Yes	No	
1	3	1	This should test your readiness to accept an appointment.
2	3	1	However, trust should not be vested without good reason.
3	3	1	
4	3	1	
5	3	1	A "no" might signal a continuing focus on tactical and functional issues over leadership responsibilities.
6	3	1	
7	3	1	
8	1	3	A "yes" might suggest that you are more open to political manipulation than that you support valid compromise.
9	1	3	
10	3	1	This should test whether there is any confusion about your own role and its performance expectations.
11	3	1	
12	1	3	This should challenge your suitability for positions of responsibility and influence.
13	1	3	

Question	Score		Comments
	Yes	No	
14	3	1	A "no" might signal a likelihood of exposure to surprise political moves in the boardroom.
15	3	1	
16	1	3	This should test any tendencies to let political expediency prevail over true and independent objectivity.
17	1	3	
18	1	3	
19	1	3	This should test any tendencies to let management solutions substitute for providing leadership.
20	1	3	
21	1	3	This should test any tendencies to abuse positions of power.
22	1	3	
23	1	3	A "yes" might indicate a tendency towards the cynical manifestations of professionalism.
24	1	3	
25	1	3	
26	1	3	

Question	Score		Comments
	Yes	No	
27	3	1	This should test whether there will be a need for some preparatory work/self-analysis before joining the board.
28	3	1	
29	1	3	There are no excuses for lazy enquiry.
30	3	1	This should test your commitment to professionalism and its continuous development.
31	3	1	
32	3	1	Directors must learn the rules of the game and their associated regulatory controls and codes of practice.
33	3	1	
34	3	1	
35	1	3	This should test your susceptibility to pre-emptive moves by other interested parties.
36	1	3	
37	1	3	

Interpreting the Scores

The maximum score in this test is 111 and the minimum is 37. If you scored between 37 and 60 you should challenge all your natural instincts before embarking on a programme of preparation. Do not be put off. Most people can make it as competent directors as all objective points of view have a relevance in the boardroom and common sense is a directors' greatest attribute.

If you score between 61 and 84 you should have many of the basic requirements in place and good preparation will do the rest.

If you scored between 85 and 111 you probably have similar values and perspectives to the authors. Beware! We, too, are still learning and do not fall into the trap of complacency. You will still be surprised, ambushed, and worked-over by your new boardroom colleagues. Prepare well and enjoy the prospect of being in a position to make a difference.

Appendices

Appendix 1

The Transition: A Series of Contrasts

Aspect	From Executive	To Director
Authority	from Position. from Resources.	from Reputation / Respect. from Objectivity.
Responsibility	to the Board.	to the Shareholder.
Power	to Command.	to Influence.
Purpose	to Act.	to Lead.
Position	as a Senior Executive. with an Extensive Support Structure. Always Answerable.	as a *New-Kid-on-the-Block.* with a Minimal Support Structure. Always Responsible.
Skills	Exercising Decisiveness. Mobilising Training. Using Analysis.	Exercising Judgement. Mobilising Experience. Using Argument.

Continuation

Aspect	From **Executive**	To **Director**
Focus	on Task.	on Role.
	on Corrective Actions.	on Preventive Actions.
	on Tactical Issues.	on Strategic Issues.
	on Resources Deployment.	on Stakeholder Value.
Behaviour	Interventionist.	Reflective.
	Competitive.	Collegiate.
	Team-oriented.	Independent-minded.
Traps	Feeling above Challenge.	Failing to Convince
	Politically-motivated.	Retreating into a Functional Comfort Zone.
	Interference.	

Appendix 2

Summary of the Reports and Acts of Parliament which have influenced Corporate Governance in the UK

Cadbury (1992)

Scope: Checks and balances

Key Principle: ***Power corrupts; and absolute power corrupts absolutely***

Impact: Scope of Chairman's Role:
- Shareholder interests
- Compliance

Scope of CEO's Role:
- Resources
- Results

Scope of Independent Committees:
- Compliance
- Audit
- Remuneration
- Nominations

Consequence: Roles of Chairman and CEO should be separated

Greenbury (1995)

Scope: Executive Compensation

Key Principle: ***Don't put the fox in charge of the chicken coop***

Impact: Composition of Remuneration Committee:
- All non-executives

Consequence: All non-executives should be excluded from incentive bonuses and share options.

Hampel (1998)

Scope: Compliance

Key Principle: ***Compliance is not merely box-ticking***

Impact: Compliance must be:
- Integral to control systems
- Capable of being measured
- Subjected to a quantitative audit

Consequence: A qualitative assurance of compliance is not sufficient

Nolan (1998)

Scope: Ethical Standards (for the Public Sector)

Key Principle: ***Deception by omission is as unacceptable as deception by commission***

Impact:	Sets seven standards for behaviour in public life:
	• Selflessness
	• Integrity
	• Objectivity
	• Accountability
	• Openness (Transparency)
	• Honesty
	• Leadership
	Deemed to be no less relevant for business with the possible exception of selflessness
Consequence:	No hiding places from legitimate enquiry

Turnbull (1999)

Scope:	Mitigation of Risk
Key Principle:	*If it can't be measured, it can't be controlled*
Impact:	Controls must be quantitative
	Contingency planning is mandatory
	Shareholders must be made aware of all corporate risk assessments
Consequence:	No legitimate hiding places for potentially embarrassing risk

Smith (2003)

Scope: Audit Committee

Key Principle: ***Oversight should be untrammelled***

Impact: Auditors must be chosen for their objectivity

Nothing is to be outside the scope of enquiry

Nothing should be hidden from enquiry

Consequence: Confidential channels for whistleblowers need to be provided

Higgs (2003)

Scope: Role of Non-Executive Directors

Key Principle: ***Executive directors need supervision to save them from falling into the vices of conflicts of interest***

Impact: At least half the board should comprise non-executive directors

Service as a non-executive should be limited to six years

A senior non-executive should have a liaison role with shareholders at shareholder meetings

Consequence: Non-executive directors are empowered to interfere whenever executive behaviour is too cosy

Combined Code 2006 and 2008

This sets out in a convenient form the latest guidance on corporate governance and a rational summary of the codes of practice from Cadbury onwards.

Companies Act 2006

This sets out new statutory duties. The most controversial is Section 172 which *requires directors to act in a way most likely to promote the success of the company for the benefit of its members as a whole.* Section 172 goes on to list the factors to consider and introduces the concept of corporate social responsibility into company law which it defines as *the concept of enlightened shareholder value.* Whereas directors are exhorted to consider the interests of employees, suppliers, customers, the community and the environment, there is no mention of the desirability of making profits.

Walker Review (2009)

The principles of corporate governance and the Combined Code are still evolving. The Walker Review of 2009 makes recommendations for the next round of changes in corporate governance as a result of perceived failings in the finance sector which emerged from the banking crisis in 2008.

Scope: Risk Management and Reward
                 in Financial Services

Continuation

Key Principle: ***Non-executive directors need to exercise greater supervision over risk assessment and senior executive remuneration and have blocking powers to constrain the more rash and impulsive aspects of executive behaviour.***

Impact: Non-executives should chair the Risk Committee.

The Remuneration Committee should have oversight of all executive compensation and the practice of deferred bonus components should be introduced when performance outturns cannot be assessed immediately.

Consequence: Better shareholder protections should result.

UK Corporate Governance Code (2010)

Scope:
This replaces the previous Combined Code on Corporate Governance (2008). It essentially updates and simplifies previous guidance and adds some new provisions to avoid certain practices that were exposed during the aftermath of the 2008 financial sector crisis. The Code is still regarded as voluntary (to preserve flexibility) but its application will be monitored by the Financial Reporting Council (FRC). It is targeted at FTSE 350 companies but many of its provisions will apply to all companies.

(1) Key Principle: Either *comply or explain*

(2) Poor performances will not be rewarded on early termination

Impact:
Directors' contracts will adopt one year service / termination provisions and the Remuneration Committee will be expected to consider the effects of the early termination of directors' contracts resulting from poor performance.

Consequence:
Poor performances, which may result in early terminations, may also lead to the application of some claw-back provisions where bonuses may not have been earned or justified.

Appendix 3

The Courtroom Model of Advocacy

STEP	COURTROOM EXAMPLE (As set out by the Defence Counsel)
State the issue	We are here to try a case of alleged murder.
Define any unusual terms	Murder is the pre-meditated act of killing.
State the conclusions	I will show that it would have been *physically impossible* for my client to have committed the heinous crime.
Give the main support for the conclusion	He was 400 miles away at the time and was taking tea with the Archberbury. (An impeccable *alibi*)
Concede and then address all the reasons why the conclusion may be challenged	The prosecution will contend that my client was seen committing the offence, but the witness is an 85 year old woman with certified blindness in one eye. (A doubtful testimony), etc.
Restate the conclusion	It would have been physically impossible to have killed anyone at 400 miles distant.
State the recommendation	My client must be discharged.

Appendix 4

The Broadcasting Model of Reporting

STEP	BROADCASTING EXAMPLE
Set the context	The latest outbreak of civil unrest in Ruritania continues unabated.
Assess the situation	Continued disruptions will now start to have an impact on power supplies and there is an imminent threat of blackouts.
Set the challenge	Unless the authorities can resolve the underlying disquiet of the public sector workers, the economy will start to suffer from disruptions to production and exports.
Evaluate the prospects	It does not look good for the country at this point with hard-line protesters holding out for pension concessions that the state feels it is in no position to concede without an unacceptable increase in the public sector borrowing requirement.

BEYOND
THE WRITTEN WORD

Authors who speak to you face to face.

Discover LID Speakers, a service that enables businesses to have direct and interactive contact with the best ideas brought to their own sector by the most outstanding creators of business thinking.

- A network specialising in business speakers, making it easy to find the most suitable candidates.

- A website with full details and videos, so you know exactly who you're hiring.

- A forum packed with ideas and suggestions about the most interesting and cutting-edge issues.

- A place where you can make direct contact with the best in international speakers.

- The only speakers' bureau backed up by the expertise of an established business book publisher.